The Tinker M

Laura Angela Co

Table of Contents
Page

Acknowledgments 2
Chapter 1 – The Beginning of the Sinning 3
Chapter 2 – The Capture by the Baby Snatcher 24
Chapter 3 – Welcome House, Welcome Home 37
Chapter 4 – Ryan Report 56
Chapter 5 – A Magdalene Left Unseen 73
Chapter 6 – My Mother's Pursuit of Happiness 83
Chapter 7 – McAyleese Report 94
Chapter 8 – Corruption Continues 105
Chapter 9 – Sour Flowers 117
Chapter 10 – Neglected Women 123
Chapter 11 – Ireland Never Learns 127
Chapter 12 – Travelling People Buried There 146
Chapter 13 – Honour the Magdalene's 156
Chapter 14 – DNA Doesn't Lie 164
Chapter 15 – I Can't Pretend This Journey Is Over 175
References 199

Acknowledgements

During this long process of our journey of truth and fighting for justice, I have met some life-long friends. Many individuals who have touched my heart and encouraged me along every step of this journey and as much as I would love to, I sadly cannot name you all. You forever hold a special place within my heart; you all know who you are. First and foremost, I wish to acknowledge my brave mother, Mary Collins. She has always encouraged and supported my family and me. She continues to be a strong and valued member of our community. I would also like to acknowledge my wonderful partner Billy Britton who has supported me in all the emotional steps through this hard process, and throughout writing this book. He has always believed in me, listened to me reading things repeatedly to him to make sure it was completely correct. Thank you, I love you so much. Also, to my adored children Angel, Amelia and Anastasia who inspired to write this book, so their history is always there for them to know. I love you all so much. May this book be the beginning to having our history be uncovered and the truth be exposed for us and all the travelling community. In addition, I would like to acknowledge my brothers Craig and Anthony. Lastly, I thank Julia, my sister in-law. I love and appreciate all of you for being in my life; you mean so much to me.

Chapter 1.
The Beginning of the Sinning

My name is Laura Angela Collins. I'm an Irish traveller who was born and raised in London by my religious mum, Mary Collins. She is a survivor of an abusive Irish industrial school run by the Sisters of Mercy where she stayed from the age of two and a half to eighteen. My mum Mary was also a child resident and visitor of St. Vincent's Magdalene Laundries in Cork which was run by the Religious Sisters of Charity.

While growing up in London, it was just my mum, my brother Craig who was a quiet reserved child who was full of fun and mischief, my little brother Anthony who was the cheeky joker of us three. We weren't wealthy, we were a very small family, but we had love given in by buckets from my mum growing up as children, although she was very strict, she wouldn't harm a fly and hates witnessing any form of violence. She was very gentle and would always encourage us to seek out for our dreams.

My father Nigel however was the complete opposite to my mother. He was an abusive alcoholic who would abuse my mum and without my mum's knowledge was also abusing her three children behind her back. He would send my mum into work with bruises on her eyes, he would aggressively attack her in front of us while my mum was screaming for us to go up the stairs so we didn't witness the horrid treatment in which was being inflicted onto my mum. My mum accepted his gruesome treatment, but little did my dad know by touching a child in front of her, that would be the straw that would break the camel's back.

One lovely September morning we was celebrating my eldest brother Craig's birthday, he was given his presents and the house was decorated; food was laid on top of a table cloth on the table in our kitchen. My dad would go crazy over the smallest of things. I cannot recall what set him off on this occasion, but he viciously hit my brother and ripped the cloth from the table. My mum saw everything; all my mums hard work was on the floor; the cake and food was all smashed to pieces – a symbol to represent his own family in which was smashed physically and emotionally by him. My mum stood coldly in front of my dad while my mums childhood filled with abuse flashed before her eyes. My young body was frozen silent in fear, just able to flick my eyes from the floor to my dad not knowing what my dad's next move would be.

My eyes quickly raced over to my mum's face who had a look on her face in which I had never seen before, a look of pure hatred. It took seeing my dad hit my older brother Craig on his birthday for her to completely break after all he put her through, she could take year of abuse, but she was not going to have her children abused. She sharply turned to the wall while she was screaming at him to get out. She then reached out and grabbed her beautiful plates she had put on the wall of our kitchen with pride – something in which she would always shout out to us about when slamming the living door as she feared them failing and breaking but now, she was chucking her adored plates she once hung with pride straight towards his head. I had never seen my mum in this animalistic state, defending her babies from the danger in which for years unknowingly they had been in, she just believed the abuse was towards her. My father used to give us sweats and hugs while telling us not to tell our mum after just physically assaulting us, we couldn't bare anymore arguments so kept silent. Loud sounds of smashing and my mum's screams filled the three-bedroom house we all shared in a quiet part of the woods, yet the loudest sound always felt like it was coming from inside my little chest. One plate shattered to pieces on the wall behind my dad that had just narrowly missed his head. "Get out, get out!", she screamed over and over while between each sentence was taking big uncontrollable breaths. My dad quickly turned to the door and slammed it behind him as he left. The last plate hitting it just as it closed shut as my mum fell to her knees on the floor and howled to us, "I'm so sorry!".

My brothers and I were in shock, not from the display, my dad made us witness worse, but we couldn't understand how that came from my gentle mum. We all asked ourselves, "Where did that come from?". We were puzzled. Not once did my mum push, hit or even poke him in all the years he abused her. However, seeing my dad abusing a child lit something within her; that was when he finally left the family home although he would continue to harass our family for a good while after that horrific incident.

My mum was fighting her own secret battle as the Ryan report was taking place, fireworks for year 2000 flew up into the sky as we watched huddled in the cold as a family of four over the river Thames, "a new year" so we thought but life never seemed to get easier for my family. We were a family in London living in a house who truly shouldn't have been there, my mum fled something terrible in Ireland, many people left Ireland in search for work, my mum left her loved hometown for no other reason but fear.

So, my father or even London Town is not what this is about nor is it where the story begins for us. It's a far darker story than my childhood. London is certainly not where it will all end, nor is it where it had started for us although it somewhat played a part in the early days as the British was those who brought over the regime of the institutions to Ireland using the poor law, they brought with them the religious orders and then after they made Ireland like them, left them to it, to go on to commit some horrendous crimes. The first Magdalene laundry was opened in white chapel London.

This story goes deeper. Where under the ground of Irish soil lied an out of use sewage tank filled to the brim with baby carcasses and neglected mass graves, spreading around Ireland with the bodies of those they neglected to death within the institutions. It's a story of a genocide, secrets, betrayal and a string of a cover ups. Effecting so many and extending over many years and sadly it widely effected my family, lets me go right back to the very start, as far as I can possibly go.

In the 50's and 60's my nan Angelina Collins, a big brown eyed, dark haired gentle woman was cohabiting with Patrick Ward for fourteen years. They were very happy minimalists. Little did they know; their family was soon to become targets of a horrid regime in attempt to "cleanse" Irish society. This evidently tore their family apart.

The Wards were from Tuam, Galway, while the Collins were from Mayo. Together in partnership with their children, they would travel all the cobble roads of Ireland in search for their next settlement at an area that would bring work.

Irish travelers although predominantly English speaking, we have our own secret language taught on through the younger generations by the elders in our community, the language is referred to as "Shelta" also known as "Gammon" or "Cant". A research study was conducted and published in 2017 which showed Irish Traveller's as a distinct group which occurred long before the Great Famine a genetic analysis shows, which went against common opinion, the study also indicated that while Traveller's originally descended from the general Irish population, they are now very distinct from it which made Irish travelers allegeable for ethic minority status, which was granted in year 2017.

Gypsy and Traveller prejudice are still one of the most accepted forms of racism within our society today and it began many years ago, which widely effected so many families such as mine. I even receive it being someone who puts myself out their publicly and proudly as an Irish traveller and have had some vile comments made on behalf of my ethnicity. Only recently a candidate running to be president of Ireland who I'm not going to dignify with naming had risen drastically in the polls due to using comments and the prejudice driven towards our community in which has always been welcomed by governments. On a whole still today wider society are very hostile towards the traveller community and at many times we have been untrustworthy of them for the reasoning you'll all soon to find out but we never wanted it to be that way nor do we wish for it to continue, we have always wanted acceptance and to work with all members of society to make a better society for all those within.

My grandad's family applied to buy land off the council for a site; many travelling people were rejected in their applications. Evidently, travelling families ended up camping on unauthorised sites or road sides. They were just looking for better lives for them and their children. They had nothing else available to them to continue their lifestyle and traditions which was something the Irish government wanted and set out to eradicate.

My nan and grandad were one of those many people who were made to camp from road side to road side. They had three children all of whom were girls who would all eventually be snatched from the road side and either imprisoned in an institution or illegally adopted. It resulted in my nan being locked away in one of their many prisons for attempting to save what was left of the family she had.

In 1931, an anonymous letter was sent to the Irish Times with the subject line, "Tinker Menace".

The letter signed, 'Pro Brono Publico' was tilted 'Tinkers children':

"It is true that these little children are dirty to the last degree, ignorant of the humblest amenities of civilised life, of all things that are taught to little children in their national schools and above all ignorant of God. Their present condition is bad, but what of their future if our only consideration is to rid ourselves of this nuisance of their presence? This is a matter for the state. Surely no Christian government should allow a heathen community to continue unchecked in its country. The only means I see to rid the whole country of the nuisance is to take the children two years and upwards, from all vagrant tinker camps, and to place them in nursery homes, where they will be taught and trained in all those social and moral principles which go to making of decent citizens. After school age the girls should get a course of domestic training to equip them for domestic work, and the boys at fourteen years of age should be passed on to the industrial school. In this way, a generation or two should see the last 'tinker menace" and in its stead our farmers and holders would have at their command a supply of well trained and efficient workers."

-Pro Bono Publico 1931

The author envisioned a regime where authorities of state & church work in concert to eradicate the primitive tinker population. The proposed technique aims for total separation between adults and children, the latter perceived as empty vessels to be filled with values and habits of "decent citizens" and "efficient workers" Nazi Germany gives the most extreme example here, with Roma one of the two groups soon be targeted for extermination on racial grounds.

A lesser known case was in Sweden, where even as Pro Bono Publico penned his or her letter, a group known as tattare (travellers) became targets of an emerging eugenics regime organised around practice of sterilisation. (Broberg and Tydén 1996)

The type of intervention proposed by Pro Bono Publico in Irish society was already being implemented in Australia with the complicity of the religious orders, with aboriginal children removed from their natural parents under the White Australia programme, through mixed persuasion and coercion. (Bird, 1993)

While there would be further calls for intervention in Ireland (Helleiner 2000: 71), the dominate techniques for normalisation would combine the themes of "rehabilitation" and "settlement" both articulated by the logic of child rescue.

During the 1950s the terms "tinker", "itinerant" and "vagrancy" were used interchangeably, with the theme of child rescue treading them together. During July of 1951, the minister for justice was asked "if he was aware of the loss and inconvenience caused to dealers.

The minister replied that "he was aware that vagrants are a source of annoyance and loss to farmers". But explained that he held out no prospect of "a satisfactory system control". James Dillon intervened by proposing Garda authorities be instructed to not allow itinerants to camp on trunk roads. "Lest their children be knocked down by passing motorists". The justice minister agreed stating, "I think the protection of children necessary with the exchange concluded by deterring the matter to Gardaí. Saving children was nonpartisan, normatively desirable and politically neutral – it operated on the motion of universal moral good."

In 1960, the first ever commission on Traveller's had been established it was published in 1963. It was called the commission of itinerancy. This document is out of print and almost unavailable.

The Commission on Itinerancy was established in June 1960, with the following terms of reference:

1.) To enquire into the problem arising from the presence in the country of itinerants in considerable numbers.

2.) To examine the economic, educational, health and social problems inherent in their way of life.

3.) To consider what steps might be taken:

a.) To provide opportunities for a better way of life for

itinerants

b.) To promote their absorption into the general community

c.) Pending such absorption, to reduce to a minimum the

disadvantage to themselves and to the community resulting

from their itinerant habits.

(4). To make recommendations.

The following were appointed members of the Commission:
Hon. Mr. Justice Brian Walsh, 'a Judge of the High Court (now
a Judge of the Supreme Court) who was also nominated to be
Chairman of the Commission; George Claxton, Vice-President
for' Leinster of the National: Farmers' Association; Revd. G.
Thomas Fehily, Director of the Dublin Institute· of Catholic
Sociology; Chief Superintendent Thomas S. McDonagh, Garda
Siochana (now retired from the Garda SiocMna); Matthew
Macken, County'Manager for Counties Carlow and, Kildare;
Dr. Maurice S. McParland, County Medical Officer of Health

for County Donegal; Dr. John B. O'Regan, Chief Medical Officer, Dublin Health.

There was not one member of the travelling community on the board. Everything in the report doesn't look at the problems Traveller's face, but the problems they are causing.

Some of the report stated:

"In present circumstances, its economically impossible for most itinerant families to remain in one district for the period of the school year. The application of such provisions could only result in most itinerant children being 'taken from their families and placed in institutions. Itinerants are very attached to their children and the evil social consequences and the suffering which must follow such a: policy would far outweigh the advantages" of an education imposed in such conditions with its lasting legacy of bitterness. Indeed, such a "solution" of the itinerant problem generally has been suggested to the

Commission-not with a view to education as such, but based, on the belief that a separation of parents and children would, result in the children growing up outside the itinerant life, and that thus, in one generation the itinerants as a class would disappear'

"For those who continuously wander compulsory school attendance should only be enforced when their economic condition has been ameliorated to the extent that there remains no sufficient excuse for their not remaining in one area in education in which suitable education is. In the view of the Commission an educational policy for itinerants can only be successful if it is one which aims at catering for those who have been induced to, leave the wandering life and for those who are likely to do so."

"23. Subject to the recommendation in paragraph 22, the Commission are satisfied existing legislation, including Section

118 of the Children Act, 1908, if enforced, is adequate. It is recommended that the statutory provisions should be enforced."

"Once that much progress has been made the elimination of the other causes of friction could be undertaken with every expectation of success and without perhaps the necessity for the continued invoking of the punitive and prohibitive legislative measures recommended in this report. It is felt that a strict enforcement of the law, at least in the early years, would have a salutary effect on the itinerants who, with their usually realistic outlook on life, would soon have a greater respect for the rights of the settled population once they realised that the authorities were serious about the enforcement of the law and that the consequences of disregarding it on either the criminal side or the civil side could not be avoided."

A later report in the Connacht Tribune shows how the theme of child rescue came to articulate the assimilatory logics of adsorption and rehabilitation.

There should be no delay in undertaking the work of rehabilitating the itinerant class. It will, no doubt, be heartbreaking and at times exasperating work. They will not be willing pupils when it comes to introducing them to the age of 60s. Nevertheless, work spent saving the life of a child is well spent. (Connacht Tribune, 1964)

Angelina's and Patrick's family roaming and camping on the side of the roads in those times was very brave as it brought not just dealing with the harsh Irish elements but also with its systems set up to separate travelling families.

The state inspectors (I.C.P.C.C) and the nuns would stroll around inspect and patrol camp sites, through their inspections they would take unmarried women and children on to institutions leaving the men in the confinement of the camps. In hope that through the use of linked institutions such as the Magdalene laundries, industrial schools and county homes which were once workhouses and mother and baby homes. They were hoping to be able to cleanse society of the travelling people and in time completely eradicate the community. Magdalene laundries also known as Magdalene asylums were places in which the state could send women to, as well as their families. They claim they were houses for "fallen women" and repeat offenders of giving birth outside of marriage. But what people are not aware of is some of these women were part of families like mine. Who were hunted down by the state and as my mum says "had their children snatched from the side of the road" for admission so that we were no longer a menace to society.

My nan escaped a county home run by the sisters of mercy. This is just one of many institutions run by an order named in the child abuse inquiry (Ryan report) excluded and not named in the current mother and baby home commission in which is looking into just fourteen mother and baby homes and four county homes. The report's publication date has been put back and extended three times over the past couple of years, when the terms of reference was finalised in 2015. Although it was in the middle of the pouring rain, my nan would have had such a urge of fear and knowledge to get away that she escaped miles away from the county home they put her and my mother into. They tried to flee to tuam back to her family, but on her journey with her toddler aged just two. She was stopped by the garda (Irish police) and her future was taken away. For 27 years she was locked away to slave out the rest of her days.

Chapter 2.

The Capture by the Baby Snatcher

Angelina's eldest child was Margaret Collins. She also had big brown eyes and dark hair. In fact, all of Angelina's children looked exactly like their mother. Patrick and Angelina's middle child was my mum Mary and their youngest was little baby Teresa. Margaret was a headstrong 14-year-old who we were informed by an elder in our community that at the time, she was pregnant. Her mother was also pregnant. On March 21st, 1962, Margaret went for a midday walk alone along the road down from the camp. While walking, she was picked up by the cruelty man and taken to the Sunday wells run by Good Shepard's laundry in Cork.

The cruelty man was what Irish Traveller's would refer to the I.S.P.C.C state inspectors as they were feared throughout the travelling community and was known to steal the children.

There were many stories going around the sites during these times of how they snatched travelling children for no reason other than using their recommendations made to the commission of itinerancy or a simple recommendation from a nun or priest. The inspector's job was to put them into religious run institutions to beat their ethnicity out of them and to forever despise and dissociate from their community. Sadly, that is what happened to my mum. There are cases where several generations were affected by their regime.

The report from the I.S.P.C.C (The cruelty men) in regard to my mum and nan said:

"I interviewed the mother of the children today. She told me she was married to Patrick Collins, an itinerant and that she was expecting another baby. The girl Ann (Margaret) Collins was in the county home, having run away from her mother. She agreed to let inspectors take this girl to the Good Shepard's Cork. I again had a talk with the mother. We were not satisfied that she was married. After some time, she admitted that she was not married. She is of low intellect. She was camped near Castlemartyr with people named Ward. Also, of itinerant stock. The mother of the Collins children said that the girl Ann (Margaret) was 14 years last September and was born in Tralee and was confirmed in Dungarvan and taken to the Good Shepard's convent this evening."

By using the records, it seems they left my nan for eight whole months even though they claimed neglect in their report but no evidence of it, other than regarding their living circumstances. Why leave a pregnant woman in the care of a child after admitting her eldest to a laundry if she was neglecting them? The reports even contradict this statement by saying all the children were well nourished and didn't have any bruises.

After the eight months passed, another report was made and it states that on January 3rd, 1963 Angelina was back where her eldest daughter was taken on the morning of March 21, 1962 and was found begging right outside the county home where she was given shelter. Two days later she was found with her two-year-old Mary trying to get towards Tuam without money to return to her partner Patrick Ward. Angelina lied in the first report claiming that his surname was Collins to avoid getting caught by having children without being married.

Amidst the pouring rain on her journey of escaping miles away from the county home she was put in, the Garda stopped her and brought her and her daughter back to the county home. From there, this sealed my nan's and mum fate and they were both sent to the laundry. A record states my mums last place of residency before being transferred on to the industrial school. St. Vincent's Magdalene laundry in Cork in which was further supported by accounts, but they also support this document with their written document stating the child was sent to an unnamed convent in Cobh. However, they don't say the convent was in fact the convent to the laundry; they doctored their reports such as saying my aunt ran away, when in fact she was pregnant, and they took her. The lack of detail in previous reports have made mine and my mums' journey of truth even more difficult.

Another report written on the January 14th, 1963 said,

"Dear sir. Please note that I intend to make an application for the committal of the above-named child to Cobh industrial school, at Cobh district court, on the 27.1.63 on the grounds of having a parent not exercising proper guardianship. The mother of the child is Mary Collins an itinerant."

The above is another example as to how bad they were with producing the records as it's my mum who is called Mary, not the mother like they stated. In addition, they refer to my mum by her middle name, Teresa.

It continued with:

The latter arrived in cork on February 1st, 1963 with her child Teresa and took shelter in Midleton co. Cork. She told me that she came from the Tuam area Co, Galway where she was camped with people named Ward. She admitted that she was not married and was cohabiting with a man named ward, also an itinerant. She has a total of three children of the association, Ann (Margret) Collins aged 14 in good Shepard's convent cork and Margaret (Bridget) born and later abandoned. Mary Collins intended to travel back to Tuam with her child Mary on the 5/1/63 without necessary money for the fare to risk and in the most inclement weather. The MO Midleton hospital certified that this mother was unfit to have the custody charge or care of her child Teresa Collins and advised be placed in care. The child was given shelter in Cobh convent. The mother is still in the county home, Midleton. My hon. Sec. believes that the responsibility of the child rests with Galway county council seeing the mother Mary Collins resided in that area up to

January 3rd, 1963 according to her version. Mary Collins is illiterate obvious to anyone, she is unfit to have care of any child. I would be thankful for an early reply to my letter with your views."

Our family know this to be untrue regarding taking my mum to Cobh convent for shelter and regarding my nan staying in the county home as she and her mum were transferred together. Onto the laundry as two nuns who knew my mum as a child in the laundry had also said to my mum and in my presence the night, she was taken from my nan in a car from the laundry car park she tried to smash the place up and had a break down. My mum was brought to the laundry with my nan and stayed with my nan until the order was placed by the court against my mum.

Even working residents of the laundry remember the night her daughter was taken from her and not just that but as previously stated, we have a record that states my mums true address before being put into the industrial school which was St. Vincent's. In the document, it also states my mums date of birth is July 30th, 1960. They purposely wrote wrong information down as a tactic to make sure they never found their relatives.

She was in fact born on the July 13th, 1960 and didn't have a birth certificate up until to a few years ago. We have no records for this unnamed convent. Where had my mum been for over that whole month as they stated in this record? It sadly again was not the truth. Further along the journey, my mum and I would find out that many things both the state and church would end up saying would be not so truthful. Once a very catholic family, who attended church every Sunday, would end up questioning their religion and fighting those within it for what's right.

My mother stayed with Angela up until this point at the laundry and if she didn't like the other written record states, it brings to question, where was she? They managed to mention all the names of the convents they put my nan and aunt into but in the written document they just state the baby was taken to the Cobh convent. Yet later in freedom of information, it states that her address before being admitted to the industrial school was St. Vincent's convent in Peacock Lane, Cork. It's been very hard to make any sense of their records all throughout this process.

We don't have a response from the Galway county council to this letter above but we do know from other documents that just one month later February 15, 1963, Mary Teresa Collins appeared before the Cobh district court. The court ruled that the 2 and half year-old girl should be committed to St. Coleman industrial school in Rushbrook Cobh. She was brought there on February 27th, 1963 and was designated number 5 by the religious order- The Sisters of Mercy. She stayed there for the next 15 years of her life, suffering beatings and humiliation while all the time being taught to hate her mother.

My mum Mary said:

"They must have hated her because she had illegitimate children and she was a traveller too I was beaten because of her, they told me she was dirty itinerant just like me. They taught me to hate her they took her from me and then taught me to hate her. They beat it into me. My time there was full of fear. A lot of children got beatings there. I was getting beaten because of my mother. I was beaten a lot for also snoring. I would be asleep and taken from my bed and stripped naked. They would stretch me across the table in the washroom. Pillows were put over my head and big girls held me down while I was beaten. There was a farm about five minutes from the home. Many nights I was beaten and taken up there. There was a pigsty there with four fat pigs. They were very smelly. I used to scream at them not to leave me there. I didn't know what I had done. But I kept saying I'm sorry. Later in the night when all the other children were asleep, someone would come back. I remember going back into the home when it was dark and getting into my bed"

In a description of her terror to a London doctor two decades later, my mum spoke about hearing the latch of the pigsty closing and starting to scream. The door would remain locked. The medical report recorded that she would be left there as she was afraid of pigs and would cower in the corner. "I was very afraid of the black cat they had in the shed with the coal. The shed used to be fill up with coal and the cat slept there. I was put there a lot. I would scream when they put me in there. This always happened after homework or reading. I'd be slapped on my face really hard for not getting something right. It was so hard my neck would hurt. I used to go to schools with scratches and bruises on my face on some occasions in the institution, I would break out in sores and spirits would be put on them. Then they would get scissors and cut each sore off my body. I was howling and begging them to stop. They told me it was the dirt coming out of me. My body was paralyzed with pain. They then wrapped me in bandages, and I wore newspaper over my bandages to stop me from scratching them. I was locked away in the dormitory until I healed. I could hear birds singing outside the dormitory and in this, I found a brief measure of peace."

Children in industrial schools were also used for child labour, however, that's hardly been acknowledged. They would be sent out on their summer to be baby sitters and cleaners. Their weekends were full of chores and making things for the church to sell as "charity". Children worked in the laundries that were filled with big machinery. They were made to even care for the younger children. They had no freedom.

They were child slaves and on the day the inspectors would attend, they would make them get out the decent bedding with no stains and then as soon as they left, they would put the stained sheets back on. These orders fully knew how to fool everyone to continue to get the funding they were receiving from the state. The state and the public were aware, but everyone was either too scared or was profiting so they didn't care to speak up.

Many times, as a child, my mum craved to be safe and had a strong will to make that her mission. She went to Cobh with other girls from the home and sailors were there and they begged them to take them away. The girls spoke up, they tried to tell the Garda about the abuse in these homes that was inflicted on them by the church. They didn't listen, didn't care and they still don't.

Chapter 3.

Welcome Home, Welcome House

My mum would jolt up in the middle of night, soaking wet, the screams racing around her head, the fear of the beating still apparent as she rises, dreams of her mother, her sister Margaret's face reappearing in the night, the words of her letters spinning around her as if she was experiencing it all again, although over 400 miles away in London with her children, my mum could never escape, the scars she carries on her skin are sadly another forever reminder like so many other aspects.

Margaret use to write to my mum in the industrial school while she was in the Sunday wells good Shepard's cork, when my mum would get these letters, they would read them out loud in the industrial school, call her dirty and humiliated my mum in front of the other children.

They would say how her sister couldn't spell and she was stupid. After the reading and insults my mother would be beaten by the matron in front of the children. My mum hated getting these letters from her sister. Like they made her hate her mum she hated her sister, yet she hated everything to do with her blood as she hated and despised herself. This is how they completely broke these children which left long lasting effects on them as adults.

Her sister one day wrote a letter and attached a picture of herself the matron showed it to my mum and they humiliated her, they kept the picture. I personally would love to have a picture of my aunt and it pains me to think we never will, so that pain must be worse for my mum.

My mum hated any form of violence and couldn't stand to witnessing any form of it even in reenactments. As young children, we all would be sitting in our living room and an

Eastenders Christmas special would be on after a morning of church and a day of festive treats and Phil Mitchel would be just about to fly his fist into someone as she screams "violence, turn it over! Turn it over!" While covering her eyes with her hands as she shakes. "I can't watch violence! Please. Turn it over NOW!"

One show my mum loved to watch was X Factor, While being cozy on the sofa with a pack of After eight mints, we would sit down and watch those with talent and those many without, myself and mum was always close, we loved enjoying music together and watching shows but sometimes I feel she looks at our relationship and sees all she couldn't have with her mother which causes a deep routed continuous circle of pain. One-night Shayne ward walked on the X Factor stage, my mum expressed how much he looked like my older brother Craig. I agreed he was dark. It then flashed to his mother Philomena Joyce. My mum expressed how she thinks they could be related. The night he was in the finals, my mum said I could vote for him once, I ran to the stairs where the phone was plugged in the wall and punched his number into the phone excitedly – this was the first occasion my mother had ever allowed me to vote. The automatic message gave thanks to me for my vote and like the Laura I have always been I took mile and made it into a marathon. I processed to call the number again and again until the lines were closed. When he won, we all jumped for joy for Shaynes success.

Myself and brothers always knew our mum was brought up in what she called a "children home run by nuns" but these institutions was no homes and deserves no such title, even in the comforts of my mother's own safe home around her family it was always lingering over her, many nights I would walk into my mums room as a little girl with piles of files & loose paper work around her while she was in floods of tears, I would swing open the door and she would be sniffing while turning away as if to be ashamed, invasive with her "I'm okay love" in response to me asking what's wrong, gathering together her piles of papers that she had got a pen to viciously scribbled over to remove the words itinerant or no fixed adobe. She had a big sliver trunk with a lock on it in which she would keep masses of paper work.

I would jump up and sit on my mum's bed while she told me all she would be feeling, well at that age so I thought but there was so much more to slowly seep out from the wounds that could not be hidden and together little at that time was we aware, we were going to enable ourselves to expose the full extent to what they tried to cover up.

From as early as I can remember my mum has been trying to gain justice for all that happened to her, her family and those alike, so her upbringing had never been a secret, although we weren't aware regarding how bad the extensive abuse and crimes was. We was always told the truth. However, we were made to keep the truth regarding where my mum came from and what our ethnicity was due to the shame they beat into my mum and the fear, we knew we was Irish Travellers but we was never allowed to tell anyone, I learned for myself as to why she carried this fear. It was very lonely for myself and brothers going to school and not being allowed to speak regarding your history while knowing and when I did confide in a friend, I was bullied for something I couldn't help nor change, I became very withdrawn and would feel angry when I would hear my fiends talk down about my community and use racist terminology such as "Pikey" and "knacker" words in which I would have to face many times in my life . For a very long time we was given one half-truth so our Christmas Day was not ruined with depression as children while my mum dragged herself through with grief and reoccurring flash backs but as kids myself and brothers we would roll our eyes at her requests with a lack of understanding thinking she was making us miss all the juicy bits on the tv in which we couldn't join in and speak with our friends about the following day in school, not that it probably would have helped, I always felt somewhat detached to those in the wider community who was not in my small family circle.

As children, my mum would let me attend survivor meetings with her, I would sit in the corner with my drawing pad which my mum brought to keep me distracted, while watching her being greeted by many survivors, whom many I saw as family, sadly many who has now passed because of alcohol, suicide or natural death. I was very mature for my age but very ignorant towards wider society while growing up, such as I wasn't really aware regarding politics, I couldn't form an understandable written sentence, I wasn't a popular child, I was the complete opposite, I was badly bullied in the schooling my mum put me in and sadly from this I learnt very little.

However, I thrived in the sector of the arts such as acting, drawing, music and dancing regardless of my lack of confidence and anxiety within it, it was something I actually did well in compared to English and Maths. I also suffer with dyslexia and with PTSD like mum does but due to my dad and other reasons, so I was very withdrawn as a child but in the company of adults I always felt I could come out and be who I truly was and say what I truly thought.

So, within the survivor meetings, observing from such a young age, it gave me a further insight as to why it all felt too much for my mum sometimes and while among the adults I fit in with regardless of being the one after the meeting sitting near the bar with a lemonade and pack of salt & vinegar crisps, while the adults had glasses of alcohol, but among it all, as different as so many aspects were for us all, among my strong mum, the people of understanding, I always felt at comfort.

When we would fly over to cork to stay in the welcome house to be among more of those who understood, cared and loved my family which we did regularly, it was always such a happy event, but on the flight over with three mischief children it was always a stressful event for my mum but we always had a great time but we always faced some form of problems on the way such as one time on our way over one of our passports expired, we begged the man who was telling us at Heathrow the bad news, who couldn't possibly do anything even if he did try. Like the children we were, disappointed after all excitement, we couldn't help but all cry, but my mum wasn't going to let us down, she never did. We hadn't even left the airport before she booked ferry tickets, before we all knew it, we were overjoyed again regarding our long couch journey to the ferry and a long coach ride on the other side once we got to Ireland by boat, it was all so worth it.

Another time we tried to come over we actually made it on the flight and got through the other side at cork airport overjoyed but they sent our suitcase on another plane, we had to wait until they brought it back a few days later which during the time my mum went to penny's and got us all some new clothes to run around cork in, we laughed it off and got on with our holiday and was lucky that another survivor took my mum down in a car to collect it a few days later.

The welcome house was amazing while growing up for myself and brothers. It gave us the family we had taken. A lovely lady in charge of the kitchen she would do the most amazing Irish fry ups. She even baby sat us for my mum one night, which my mum never ever got to do while in London as we had no extended family while growing up. Other than an aunt who was adopted who I met a handful of times on special occasions, she would always promise and make dates to see us, we would be all dressed up waiting for her to come but she would always end up letting us all down on the day arranged after us children and my mum being so excited to see her.

The survivors in welcome house had a connection to each other, they understood each other's journeys, they cared for us so much as I believe as children, they were treated badly so they give so much back like my mum always had to others and us.

They would support my love when I was younger in performing arts and would encourage and help me put on many different shows in the living room of welcome house, which we all got a lot of laughs from. Every person there was like the family we had taken but most of all the welcome house gave us a way to affordably be in the country we love during the Ryan report was taking place, the country my mother was forced out off due to their systems of slavery and abuse.

The welcome house was there while my mum was dealing with what was happening within Ireland and it had lower rates for survivors staying, if I'm being fully honest on the whole experience it had one incident which was dealt with quickly, such as a man became very drunk and when he returned he was refused entry, he lashed out at another survivor called Robert who I'm still great friends, while us children sat in the living room trying to not look outside the door to draw attention to ourselves. But it had far more good than bad, that was the only one incident I remember. When JJ, a fantastic survivor who will forever stay in my heart RIP JJ, would be driving us back to the airport I would look out the window and cry and tell my mum to leave me there.

I adored Ireland and the welcome house. It was truly like our second home. Survivors there they really were like family they kindly brought us to the aquarium and to an amazing zoo in Ireland, they would buy us toys and we had a little toy box in the corner of the living room, where we would leave all our stuff for the other children who may come along and for when we would return.

JJ was in the horrid Christian brothers, he was such a kind man and so lovely to all us kids, he had amazing magic skills I will never forget JJ. JJ one day brought a horse and wanted myself and brothers to name it, I will never forget that day as I was stuck in mud up to my knees fearing for my life over a bull as I was wearing red (I only know now it's a myth) but anyway, my brothers and JJ encouraged me across and when I did, there we saw a stunning white horse which we agreed to call snowflake, people like JJ brought so much light in the darkest of situations. JJ sadly passed away, I would really love to know where he lays and place a pack of cards on his grave side and pay my respects but like my aunts and grandads graves it's still unknown.

I would always moan to my mum while back in London by saying I'm more accepted in Ireland, I was being bullied in the schools in London and I would say that the schools there in Ireland was better, really, I had no idea, I just wanted so badly throughout my whole childhood to be there and live there as that's what felt right when I was there. I was a happier child in Ireland, I was in a child's ignorant bliss.

Now my opinion as a grown women has shifted a little, I want to be there for my nan and for when my mum needs me, I want to gain the justice my family rightfully deserves which we have been fighting for two decades but as I get older, like my mum I know and understand while things are not resolved the pain is too much to even settle there and being there causes a load of old wounds for my mum to open and for me to see, it creates honestly anger and resentment.

My mum has been fighting for deserved justice since the 90s, I was six! I'm now twenty-five, throughout my life it's consisted of survivor's meetings and seeing how the government treats and scams its people and we are still left fighting.

The last time we travelled and stayed in Ireland to try gain our families justice that should just be rightfully given. We were left badly financially hit.

The welcome house was like a little hotel, it had many different rooms with keys, the kitchen you could use throughout the day as you pleased, including the living room and you were welcomed and among other people that understood your background, your experiences and could relate, now there is no support for survivors and their relatives who they ran out of the home country they loved. Emotionally they cannot currently return while the truth is concealed, justice is withheld, the permission of the remains of loved ones to be removed from mass graves are restricted.

I was explained what had happened to my nan as a very young child, following to that we went to Ireland to visit my nan in the mass grave she was placed in for the very first time. But before we did that, we begged my mum to show us the industrial school in which she grew up in. She hesitantly agreed and we strolled down a walk way and came to a big gothic building. My mum knocked on the door and a woman opened the it, she explained to the women she used to live there, at that point myself and brothers saw a rusty climbing frame on the land in the distance. We ran over to it over joyed without a second thought. We all climbed up, I had one leg over the bar and I suddenly jumped as I heard man's voice shout, "oi" from the window of the building. I looked up, still half balancing myself on the pole as I looked through the window, I saw a dark-haired man with children with hollow pale faces, who had no expressions on their face which was standing behind him all peering out. As I looked at him. He quickly screamed again in his thick Irish accent but this time he shouted, "Get out of here you b******s".

With my mouth, wide open I was in complete shock, while he was pinning his eyes straight though us aggressively from the window. My older brother started awkwardly laughing and quickly dismissed him. I gave a I'm not scared look and laughed to my brothers, but I couldn't help but shake, myself and little brother was still very young at the time. While on the post, I looked at his face again and gave a dirty look to match his language, "now" he uncontrollably screamed again as my mum came running down the path towards us in complete fear telling us to come down. While leaving, I couldn't understand why he just called us that for being children, I didn't know what the word meant, but after this point I started finding out, but I didn't know at the time, I just knew it was a bad word. As we walked out of the industrial school, I asked my mum why he could talk like that in front of those children behind him, let alone to children. We were never allowed to swear; my mum didn't while we grew up and I had never been sworn at by an adult unless it was by my dad. She responded with "I don't know love but it's not right" she had a flood of sadness take over the expressions of her face. You okay mum I asked? She turned to as all and said, "completely fine, don't let what happened ruin things, let's go see your nan".

When we arrived at St. Finbarr's gate, we walked down the long walk way filled with many headstones, we turned left. We then slowly approached, and we were greeted by something we didn't expect.

When we arrived, we were greeted by a dirty, grey, head stone, that towered over me. It read many different women's names, I read the headstone while wiping away dirt, we soon came across Angela's name which was put up along with seventy-two other women's names. After seeing the mass grave and my brother craig laying a flower and saying to her "when I'm older I'll come back and lay flowers on nan's grave mum," from this my mum felt she needed to do more, so we went back to Ireland as a family but this time we were on a mission.

In 2003, we had purchased a new head stone that read "Angela Collins, St. Vincent's, peacock lane, cork from 1961.

Suffering lifelong separation from her children. Until her death in 1988.

On the feast of St. Angela aged 57 years now at peace in her eternal home. Rip."

We also placed an angel statue next to the head headstone, we cleaned up the ordinal headstone and paid respects to Angela and all whom lay there.

Chapter 4.

Ryan Report, No Justice of Any Sort.

I don't remember much about the first year in Cobh, I remember at the age of seven being abused. I was about seven when a nun told me I had a mother and I was going to see her. I was told that I must not mention to the other children I have a mother. I came to believe it was something bad. I felt alone that I had this secret that I had a mother. The thought of going to see my mother sacred me. When the big day came for me to go and see her, I had no feeling about her as I didn't know what a mother was. I had never left St Coleman's to go anywhere else but school which was near the home, I didn't know how to talk or laugh as everything inside me was dead. The only thing I knew was fear. I left for the first time with matron. Her name was Bernadette, she scared me as she abused me, I never talked to her because I wasn't allowed to speak to her.

Once out of the home on the train Bernadette kicked me, I was miserable while on the train. The train stopped in cork and we walked down the town and got the number 2 bus to St Mary's road. Bernadette walked in front of me, I just followed her, I was coming to a big building with holy statutes outside.

Bernadette whispered to the nun named Sister U. Sister U looked clean all dressed in white with a heavy cross. She didn't scare me. I liked her because she looked so bright. I was sent to a room with a big round table and four chairs. It had a big clock on the wall. It was very cold. It took time for my mother to come. I sat in silence waiting for her. I could her walking down the hallway as she came down it. The door opened and it was sister U, my mother and a friend of my mother Mary Ellen Moran. My mother kept her eyes on the floor and said hello in a husky voice. She sat down so did Mary and nobody talked. My mother was staring at the table she couldn't even look at me. I didn't like the look of her eyes, they were sunk in and her movements was slow.

The matron Bernadette was kicking me under the table. She gave me an awful look. She was saying talk to your mother. I couldn't. I didn't know how to talk to her as we weren't allowed to speak with adults in the children's home. I also had difficulty in pronouncing words, and I got beaten for that. I was watching the clock go around and around. I sat there for a long time not understanding what I was to do or how I was to react. It was time to leave. My mother stood and said goodbye. The matron never spoke to me all the way back. She had no expression on her face.

When the matron got me back to the home, she marched me in hitting my head and throwing me to the ground. She brought me into the dressing area and stripped me naked. I was struggling when she was hitting me, so she grabbed me and laid me down naked and I was stretched, and I was screaming as she was hurting me while stretching my hand behind my back. She called the big girls in to hold me down. They got pillows and put it over my head so she couldn't hear my screaming. I said sorry Bernadette I will not do it anymore, I never knew what I did, she kept tell me I was like my mother. I remember giving up laying there and not being able to breathe. When she had finished the beating, she threw me of the table. My body hurt, I just wanted to sleep. I couldn't walk. She got the big girls to take me to the coal house. That is where the black cat stayed. I felt cold there all alone. She closed the door and locked it. I fell asleep, she came back when it was dark and made me go to bed.

My time at the home was full of fear. A lot of children got beatings for being there, I was getting beaten because of my mother. I would be asleep and taken from my bed for snoring and stripped naked. They would stretch me across the table in the washroom. Pillows were put over my head and the big girls held me down as Bernadette beat me. She used to hit me hard on my front and bottom. This was never done unless I was naked.

Bernadette also used to pour pots of urine over my head that we used for the toilet at night. I was asleep when this happened. It was because of my snoring and when I woke up, she reminded me I was dirty and would turn out like my mother.

On my first holy communion, I made with three other girls. I remember the matron pushing me down the stairs before I went to the church in my communion dress. I never remember one day I wasn't beaten. Bernadette was always doing something to me. She would cut my toenails very far back and they would bleed. This was very sore. I remember one of the older girls died of leukemia. I remember having to see this girl laid out. She was cold and stiff. I was told to kiss her goodbye, I panicked, and I was beaten. I thought the girl had turned into a statute. I didn't know what a dead person was meant to look and feel like.

I couldn't speak properly, and I couldn't pronounce my words properly, Bernadette would keep slapping my face until I said the word properly. It was impossible for me to say them properly, so I was beaten all the time for that. I couldn't speak properly and had my face pushed onto a desk with force. I used to have nose bleeds because of this. This happened every day after school as I couldn't learn.

There was a farm about five minutes from the home. Many a night I was beaten and taken up there. There was a pigsty with four fat pigs. They were very smelly. I used to scream to Bernadette not to leave me there. I told her I was sorry. She would lock me up there and go back to the home. I was very afraid of the pigs. I would pray to god for Bernadette to come back and get me.

Bernadette would come back when all the children were asleep. I remember going back into the home when it was dark and getting into bed. In the morning, nobody had known what happened to me that night. I was also very afraid of the black cat they had in coal house. The shed use to big filled up with coal and the cat slept there. I was put in there a lot. I would scream when Bernadette would put me in there. This always happened after homework or reading. She would slap my face really hard for not getting it right. It was so hard my neck would hurt. I use go to school with scratches and bruises on my face.

Bernadette use to cut my hair above my ears, and she was very rough with the scissors on my neck. She never treated me with any kindness. There were times when she would try and push me down in the bath. Bath time was very frightening. I had to wear the same pants for the whole week and if it was dirty, she would make me wear it over my head. I changed my pants the same night I had a bath. I lost my name in the home. I was number 5 there. I knew my name was Mary because they used it in school.

Bernadette use to make me get in a very hot bath. My feet hurt. She would scrub my body with the scrubbing brush until it was raw. She would then put chamomile lotion on it. I hated it. I think she was treating me for scabies. This would happen most nights until the scabies had cleared. There were times when Bernadette would hold my head under water, and I would struggle for breath.

I remember one day Bernadette told me I was sick, but I wasn't. I think the reason she said I was sick is the other children was being brought to the seaside. She didn't want me to go. She slapped me across the face and hit my head off the wall until I said I was sick. In the end, I said I was sick, so she sent one of the big girls to get a tablet from the medicine room. One of the big girls gave it to me and I fell asleep very quickly.

I remember being woken up then with a lot of yelling and screaming going on. People were telling me I was going to die and not to sleep. I kept dropping off and they kept slapping my face all night to stop me sleeping. They kept telling me I was going to die, I didn't want to die as I thought I was going to the devil, so I drank and drank water until the morning. I used to get sick a lot and I can remember being hit for vomiting. Bernadette would hit me and knock me to the ground, and I use to have to clean up my own vomit. My front tooth was broken by Bernadette, I had my face hit off sinks while washing my hair. She used to hurt me while washing my hair. I was always cold and lonely.

I never wanted to see my mother as I believed she brought me such pain. I wished I was treated like the other girls who didn't have mothers, I never knew my mother in anyway other way than just someone I got abused over. When I was about thirteen, I was looking in the mirror, I had to wash under my arms every day and I had my pants on. I was an innocent child one minute and then the next I was being dragged into the table by Bernadette, she was calling me a trampsmaid, a bad egg, a whore like my mother, she was hitting my breasts that hadn't developed. She was attacking my sexuality. She was trying to make me hate my body, I think she didn't want me to turn out like my mother.

She used to also be horrible to me at times, she used a black strap on me and left a mark on the palm of my hand. The stripping naked ended when Bernadette left the school. I remember being beaten most mornings by Bernadette before going to school. Before school we went to church and cleaned the children's home. I remember the floor wasn't cleaned to Bernadette's high standards and as a punishment she sent me to school with no elastic in my pants. I had to hold my pants up with the band of my uniform. My pants fell down in class. All the outside children were laughing, and I was sent off from class back to the home. I got beaten so badly by Bernadette after that. I learned to black out my feelings. I didn't have any feelings the time Bernadette was using me as a punch bag.

I wet myself every day when I was young. I had to wear rubber pants and sleep on a rubber mattress. It was cold and hard. I remember being a very quiet child who never spoke. I remember after school when I was fourteen years of age, I tried to run away, me and another girl. We went down to the pier in Cobh, there was a foreign ship in, we use to leave school to go down and talk to the sailors, they promised to take us away when the ship was leaving, we were ready to go with them but the police in Cobh turned up and took us back to the home. Sr A nearly killed me bashing my head of the iron post in the cloakroom. She told me I would have a black baby if I went with them. I didn't know what she was talking about. Another day we went down to the pier and one of the girls had a fit and fell in the water. I was in trouble again and beaten and starved and sore from the scrap.

I had to wear very tight shoes, I never had a new pair only when I had a visitor. To this day, I can't wear nice shoes as my small toe sticks up. When I didn't get my exams Sr A was very mad. I remember her pulling me by my hair and telling me I was no good and I was just like my mother and she was going to ask Sister U in St Vincent's if I could go and work in the laundry with my mother.

My mum expressed all she could to the Ryan report, the above is some of what she stated, During the time of the Ryan report in 2000, they knew regarding the laundries, the mother and baby homes, the county homes as they was all connected and people like my mum who presented themselves in good faith of gaining full justice spoke up regarding the laundries and county & mother and baby homes being the first place they was put into before being transferred to a industrial school and then followed by the laundry for those in the community who they felt had no place in the society they was trying to cleanse so they keep them for years for no crime but their identity and status.

When the Ryan report was put in place and was looking at the abuse of the children in industrial schools many people not only spoke but had in their records regarding the laundries and other institutions such as my mum but the Irish government claimed it was private and gagged a load of people based on lies and an unfair trail. While the state recommended lawyers and barristers, they were the ones to gain greatly financially.

Meaning those who took part in the Ryan report, they could never prosecute those who took the actions on them in the industrial schools and used these children for slave labour as the government put a clause that stated this which was again protecting the criminals and child abusers while giving people a small payment of hush money that didn't even included the full extent, some survivors didn't understand the full effect that this would have on everyone that then came forward with a complaint against the protected person.

The mandate of the commission was to investigate whether abuse happened, what kind of abuse happened, why it happened, how it happened and how much of it there was. This means it excluded, it was not a full investigation into all of these institutions and their mass graves sites, it was just looking at the abuse within the walls of the industrial school, the lawyers from the abuse cases made over 1 million in profit.

My mum tried to get the abuse in which happened to her and her mother in the laundry included in the Ryan report and a full investigation opened, instead they didn't listen and even failed to further take action and investigate these places mentioned to them and the abusers after the Ryan report finished. Instead they protected the abusers which many was not aware that they wouldn't at least be pursuing the people mentioned who committed abuse on children.

From the Ryan report caranua was set up, the government continued to keep control to benefit through others loss, pain and suffering and set it up so it was this way. Just like the way they set up the 50/50 deal between them and the religious orders for the Ryan report, instead of putting an independent legal office in place for survivors to take these cases to court.

Myself and many others in the community strongly believe instead of just giving survivors what was rightfully theirs during the Ryan report they put Carauna in place which had so little respect for their compensation they controlled and even spent survivor's money on refurbishing offices they planned to shortly leave from and did leave from and then they spent the money also in bars on their staff.

Their compensation within Carauna and the interest which is never spoken regarding should have been protected and only spent on the community. Even more so when they had taken away from survivor's children who need extra curriculum lessons, those children born after year 2000 was not entitled, yet they had enough of survivor's money to spend it on themselves rather than them and their children. It certainly should not have been spent for nights out with coworkers, when these children worked unpaid, gave free labour where the church benefited through these children which they do not acknowledge, and they have already lost out on so much.

Child slave labour in industrial schools is not really a focus as the abuse in industrial schools was so extreme in many cases like my mums and although many was badly abused and worked hard at such young ages, they never saw a penny for all their "charity" which was in fact child slave labour in so many cases.

Although my mum had a gagging order on her head meaning she could be prosecuted if she spoke out regarding her abusers in the industrial school, she powered on and kept fighting for justice for my nan and herself regarding the laundries as working outside their clause and using their exclusion against them, one of her abusers took her up and abused her in the Magdalene laundry. My mum was contacted by a man who knew a friend of my mum who wanted to do a documentary which my mum took part in, my mum was one of the first individuals who helped to bring awareness to the Magdalene women through the documentary called *The Forgotten Maggies,* she helped fight for the government apology to the Magdalene laundries and in 2013 after marching and protesting the streets of Ireland she helped to pressure the government to issue a halfhearted apology, she also planted a tree in remembrance of life's lost.

Chapter 5.

A Magdalene Left Unseen

Angelina after being transferred to the laundry was locked behind their doors at night and expected to use a bed pan as the toilet, she had her long hair cut up to her ears and her clothes taken and was given uniform to wear and was told she would no longer be called Angelina but Angela.

The first few days she was there her daughter was present with her, so she was somewhat calm, but a few nights later there was a problem, a big one in fact where all the residents knew regarding it. Angelina now named Angela was screaming, smashing all items in her sight, she was grabbed and being forcefully held back from the doors by nuns.

In a struggle, she was dragged to her room where she was locked behind the door, she used the bed pan given for her to use for the toilet during the night, to continuously hit the door screaming while fully knowing there was nothing that she could possibly do, she kept smashing it into the door, kicking, banging, until all her energy had drained and the room filled with silence. Covered in tears, weak and heartbroken she stumbled to the bed, she heard the door lock open, behind it was two other girls, they walked over beside Angela to comfort her one girl called Anne and the other called Mary Ellen Moran, my nan was shaking and covered in sweat, she had just lost the last of her 3 daughters as they bundled Mary in a car and drove her out of the laundry car park. The two girls comforted my nan throughout the night, stroking her wet tangled hair from her face, whispering in her ear, while holding her close, that "it will be okay pet".

Angelina's daughter Bridget her youngest daughter just a newborn baby was already being lined up to be adopted and was in foster care of the parents in which wished to adopt her. They couldn't have children and gave the life every child deserves to my aunt. While my nan was being kept in the laundry after the night she exploded, she became withdrawn and quiet, many believed after the outburst regarding her child, that it could have been her character in which just made her withdrawn or not being able to see the freedom of the road again, myself and mother would later find out they was not only giving my nan pills but also giving her brain shocking treatment which kept her in order.

For five years, the once newborn baby named by my nan as Bridget in which they claimed in reports my nan to abound, my nan was refusing to sign adoption papers for five year for, if the child was unwanted liked their doctored reports claimed, then why would she hold on to her as this shows she was wanted, it was only when they used my mum who was being badly abused in the industrial school and said if she signed the papers she can start getting visits from my mum.

Through emotional blackmail they succeeded in getting my nan to sign the adoption papers, from there at the age of seven my mum started visiting the laundry from the industrial school where she was inflicted more physical and mental abuse upon, she would be kicked and punched under the tables to speak all in which was excluded from the Ryan and the McAyleese report.

While looking through Angela's medical records it shows they neglected her to death, not only did they not know her age on every occasion they reported on her, for example in eight years, they claimed my nan only aged three, but most importantly a doctor also recommended a hysterectomy. The Catholic Church was against sterilization unless it proved to be a risk of life, although advised by doctor, they left my nan to continue to work unwell in the laundry for a whole decade, while still filling her with brain shock treatment and pills, she then bled to death within church, the cause of her death was found be ovarian cancer.

Before Angela's death her daughter Margaret had fled to Liverpool after leaving the laundry, she tried to return to Cork and took the long journey from Liverpool to Ireland to try find her mother and sisters. She went to the laundry her mother was in and they left her outside the door, she never got to see her mother, she returned to Liverpool heartbroken and that coming Christmas committed suicide on Christmas Day, we were always aware my aunt committed suicide but we weren't aware until a little older that it was on Christmas Day, that's the half-truth I referred to previously, we also do not know where she was buried.

When Angela died from neglect her remains was dumped into a neglected a mass grave with seventy-two other women in St. Finbarr's cemetery Cork, the mass grave site is owned by the religious sisters of charity. When baby Bridget was adopted My aunt, Bridget was adopted within cork and attended the school across the way from the laundry where her mum was enslaved. It's literally a stone throw away. While my aunt was attending the school, she had and still has such a beautiful voice and was part of the school choir and this school they would bring this choir into the laundry to sing to the Magdalene women and in the crowd of women was her mum Angelina. She never knew she would be singing to her mum, she didn't know who her mum really was.

My aunt had said to me:

"I knew I was adopted but believed my mum would live in a massive house with lots of money and one day she will come take her away"

Kids imaginative thinking bless her. Instead when they introduced my mum Mary as her sister and she found out who her mother was from my mum, a woman enslaved in peacock lane Magdalene laundry, the women she had known to be singing to while going up there with her school. It was honestly and understandably so very hard for her considering the lovely background her adoptive parents gave to her which my mum has always been so happy about, my mum has always said:

"I would have hated it if my little sister went through the same as me in an institution, to know she was at least protected, the only one out of us all, knowing the youngest was cared for has given me so much comfort. "

But for Bridget when informed she felt the shame that was on all the women and their children as society made it that way, which even my mum had towards her mother growing up as the nuns implemented it in the industrial school. Bridget loved my mum and loved also having someone that looked like her as she had never had that but due to the shame, she told all her friends that my mum and herself was cousins understandably as it was very hard for her to come to terms with. It still seems to be.

My mum, she didn't care at all, she was just happy to be called a cousin and having someone that looked like her and was related I remember her saying she looked like me but not like me at all. She was so pretty, she had big brown eyes, (like her) and had long hair and such pretty clothes, my mother was in owe of her beauty. There was no denying they wasn't related, they are two pees in a pod even still.

Their mother also looks exactly like them also, so cousins was the best that she could come up with at the time due to their looks. When I first met my beautiful aunt, I was shocked with how much she looked like my mum and how alike we both was personality wise.

Angelina my poor nan enslaved for twenty-seven years left without medical treatment for ten years to be dumped in a mass grave by the religious sisters of charity, while alive and suffering she would have to watch her baby daughter perform without being told that's your baby. Any mother out there I'm sure would sit there and think that could be my little girl, she looks like me. She could be one of my children.

Myself and my three daughters have this exact patterned gene that my nan has with her daughters. It's like this pattern of looking exactly alike to your mother with very slight differences, I know she would have been sitting there racking her brain out with questions and suspicion as I would have. The thought is just torture. How can a mother not know, you have the automatic connection to your children. You would just feel it I believe. They didn't just torture my nan physically but also emotionally and psychologically and used her children to do so and which also tortured and caused so much hurt for them.

My aunt cannot at all attend the mass grave where her mother lays with seventy-two other women even while in Cork, although she has tried but due to all the pain attached to the site, it's too difficult. They would have known where and who my aunt was they had all the records (as is why they managed to get my aunt and mum in contact) they certainly knew who her mother was but they were purposely dangling women's children in front of them. It's just heartless! My aunt has suffered so badly emotionally from it all. Being in the laundry and singing to what she later found out to be her mother. It's just sickening.

They made Magdalene women & their children suffer in ways that are so cruel to hurt their mothers further I believe and still none of it was acknowledged. My aunt was in the laundry with her mum as a little girl, while thinking and craving for her mum and she was right in front of her singing to her. While my nan she would have been watching while breaking inside with so many questions and lack connection to her children who was put in front of her in such cruel circumstances, but sadly they already broke her before this point.

Chapter 6.

My Mum's Pursuit for Happiness

Mary Collins, my mum grew up from the age of two to eighteen within an industrial school, she was a trouble maker, a rebel, and although she was very gentle and kind, she couldn't keep out of trouble. Mary wished for freedom, she would see the girls out of the convent and would be amazed by their pretty bracelets and headbands. She wished to have clothes that fit and shoes that wasn't so small it made her toes curl, or a normal sized blazer that didn't eat up her tiny figure.

She just wished to be a normal little girl playing in the fields, instead she was locked behind a big brown door and was made to scrub until they could see their own reflections in the chapel floor, until their knees would feel like they were about to bleed, none of the girls wore gloves to protect themselves from the products they were using at such young ages.

Mary was a care free little girl, although she was receiving physical, mental abuse and abuse against her sexuality daily, but it was a norm for her. Although they tried to beat my mums character out of her, drugged her with sleeping tablets to nearly the point of death, where they kept her up all night while slapping her face while saying "don't go to sleep your dying" and making her drink water while she screamed "I don't want to die" while fearing she would be sent straight to the devil like the nuns would say.

Regardless my mum would still go against the nun's orders and wouldn't think twice about doing so. The nuns would grow apple trees which the apples were only for the nuns to eat, my mum would climb up the highest tree hungry for real food and eat them. She would get caught most of the time, which would result in more punishment, but she also had got away with it on many occasions, so the hunger and thought of previous success brought her back.

My mum was a very popular young woman, she was the only girl within the home that had friends outside of the children's home. Riding a bike down the steepest hills in Cork with her friends was a taste of the freedom my mum never had, but my mum wouldn't let it go there.

During my mum's time in the industrial school, she was battered by objects, was stripped naked for beatings and lashings. She would be lock out in the barns at night to sleep with animals. She also couldn't speak properly because what she found out later in life was that she had two stones put up her nose. So, because she spoke weirdly, they would taunt my mum Mary and bash her head off the table.

She was also left handed, the sign of a devil child according to the nuns. So, they would attack her by making her write with her right hand and when my mum couldn't do it, the nun would bash her head of the tables. My mum feels she received worse treatment than some other girls in the industrial school as her mother was part of a travelling community and because they knew her mum could do nothing about what was happening to my mum Mary as Angela was locked up by the nuns in peacock lane, Magdalene laundry, Cork.

My mum was told at the end of her time in the industrial school that if she didn't get a job, she would have no option but to go to a Magdalene laundry where her mother was. My mum had already been entering the Magdalene laundries from the age of seven to see her mother who would be sitting at the end of the table drugged by the nuns during all her time in their "care" to keep her calm.

At this age, sadly my mum despised her mum, she would hear bad story's regarding her mum and received beatings on her behalf, they would call her a murderer, a thief. Yet later it was confirmed by Garda reports it was all lies, it was all said just to put fear in to what they called "the dirty itinerant child".

While visiting her mum she had nothing to say, she didn't know what to say, neither did Angela. So, the nuns would kick and pinch my mum Mary to try a get her to say something, but the words would never come out.

So, on the way home while they were travelling on the train with the nuns my mum Mary was abused, and she would also expect a beating once they got back to the home too. So, my mum hated the laundries, she held the shame of her mother being in there and saw how much of a shell of a person she was because of what they did to her.

My mum made sure once she left the industrial school that she would never have to enter the place that still haunts her in her sleep. The sight of a Hospital looking room, big clock, silence apart from tick, tock, tick, tock but in the silence, no one can hear the mother and child's silent sobs and streams of tears.

My mum had managed to find a job, she wasn't going to move into the Magdalene laundries, my mum was sexually assaulted in the home where she obtained work by the father, he later shot himself, she then went to another place of work with a lovely dentist who looked after her so well but sadly because of a marriage breakdown, my mum had to leave, she loved the three children she cared for.

My mum didn't want to be forced into the Magdalene laundries from losing her employment, so she fled and became homeless on London streets, alone and with no one my mum began squatting, she had no family support and was a homeless survivor. My mum was a hard worker and got a job as a cleaner she also started renting her own room and later had her three children eldest Craig Collins, Myself and youngest Anthony Collins.

My eldest brother Craig had woken up one morning and entered the bathroom, he felt faint and sick. In that moment, he violently vomited pure red blood everywhere. He collapsed, my mum heard the thud from downstairs and ran upstairs while screaming "Craig!", when she walked around the corner, she wasn't prepared for the sight she was about to walk into.

Craig was covered in blood, he was slowly getting up from the floor when he flung his body and arched it over the bath, again he violently vomited. My mum called the ambulance, she flung her sons arms on her shoulders and brought her son down the stairs. Craig lost his life in the ambulance, but they brought him back around, yet he kept falling in and out. My mum was traumatized she didn't know what was happening to her baby, she had never had this feeling before, the feeling of watching your child slowly slip away from you.

Craig was rushed into intensive care, they did everything they could to make him stable and had given him blood transfusions as he was running off 1 pint of blood as he lost so much of it. My mum was told after tests that her son had plastic anaemia, very weak and shocked Craig fainted from a lack of blood when he was told he would not be allowed to leave for a while. He landed on his face, which he spilt his lip and nose, he was then taken in for a scan on his face where they found a tumor behind his nose, which if they hadn't of found the tumor, eventually it would have spread and killed my brother. Both Craig's conditions was of rare forms.

Craig needed to have the tumor removed before having any treatment on his bone marrow. Craig needed a bone marrow transplant; my mum didn't speak with my dad and all she had for a family was her two children. The doctors said they would need to test all her children; the travelling blood line is so close and strong that we were all matches.

This was the point when my mum truly connected to her mother. My mum went home after leading her son in for his major operation, she left upset and walked home to walk her dog. On the walk back my mum felt emotional, the feeling of what her mother went through kicked in as she was experiencing it. My mum stayed two years within the hospital with her son Craig. She had no choice but to, Craig wouldn't be here today if my mum didn't stay with her son. But in front of her eyes she was slowly losing her son and couldn't be with her other two children. My mum felt the true, raw, pain, of losing her children which her mother had also experienced.

She felt angry and for the second time in her life, my mum displayed aggression. She forcefully punched the wall and in that split moment she felt a sudden rush of tranquility, something told her it was going to be okay and her son was going to make it through. She slowly walked back to the hospital to greet her son from his operation. On the walk back she felt strong, as if someone was walking with her.

During this time, my mum had to again face up to her past as she sat in a hospital room, with a big faced clock, silence apart from tick, tock, tick, tock. The only difference was, it wasn't her mum who was drugged up, but her son. She feared the nurses and feared the room throughout her two-year experience, but after a two-year struggle, Craig fought his way through his illnesses with his mum by his side, Craig sat his GCSES within hospital and he passed all the exams he took. He went on to study at one of the best university's in the UK. He married and moved America where he has a lovely wife and successful career.

After the two-year ordeal, the family was reunited, and my mum Mary finally had a full understanding of what her mother Angela had been through. My mum started working harder on behalf of her mother's justice and families. She already cared and had done a lot on behalf of what happened to her mum and herself, but she now had the strength to follow it through and the full understanding. My mum is no longer homeless and is no longer a cleaner, she lives in a 3-bedroom home and has a thriving career. It just shows, you can come from nothing and still do a lot.

Along the way people have tried to stop my mum on her quest for justice for herself and mother regarding the Magdalene laundry and county homes and all interlinked institutions but she never stops.

Chapter 7.

McAyleese Report, No Close Support

After my mum being part of the documentary the forgotten maggies and being part of a movement to gain justice. There were government cronies placed on the field to influence opinion, some groups purpose is to gather up members to then claim that theses members want this or that. When really the group leaders are paid to agree with the government and with the members counted as the "majority" to say they want what is not actually wanted by survivors themselves.

After my mum working so hard to get to the point to see the apology the government lead group refused to give my mum a ticket to the apology in the Dáil, it was only that an independent had helped my mum obtain the ticket. On the night of the apology they excluded the children of these women and the dead women laying in mass graves whose lives were taken through neglect and didn't even issue a minute's silence for all lives lost. The Magdalene women's apology was just issued to the living working residents.

It left my mother heartbroken, I sat in the UK with my partner and young baby Angel as I watched disgusted on the news, my mum called and broke down, she was in floods of tears, she couldn't understand how they was able to keep excluding people from justice.

The apology was just issued to the living working residents of the Magdalene laundries and they were not compensated like it's believed as it's promoted. They were just given their wages in which they should have already had, a pension and a medical card as they effected their health, repaying what should have already been someone's as you withheld it, is not actually compensation. There would in future be more accounts of the government group purposely excluding my mum from events. I was angry for my mum, that my nan and mum and all lives lost excluded from the apology, that they didn't even issue a minute's silence.

After the apology mum asked the order to remove her mother's remains from the mass grave by letter, she was ignored. We were getting no response. So together we set of to Dublin in Ireland, on our way out of the airport, we got into a cab and went down to a care home where we knew a nun was in who knew my mum at the time she was in the laundry as a seven-year-old. Before entering I couldn't help acknowledging how lovely the care home was, to then think of where my nan laid in the neglected site. As we approached the front desk of the care home, we gave her name and said we was here to see her, we got brought to her room and it was as if she had seen a ghost. "Oh, my Mary Teresa now why do I have this pleasure of an unexpected visit" she sat down and spoke with my mum as I looked around her room at all the holy elements she kept within it, pictures of holy figures holding children, when at this point after watching the documentary my mum was in, I knew the truth and couldn't help my thoughts further wondering.

I suddenly tuned back in when my mum mentioned my nan, "aw yes our dear Angela god rest her soul" the nun said. My heart thudded at her statement.

"I want her exhumed from the mass grave" my mum said swiftly. The lady looked very uncomfortable, "and why would you wish to do that dear, why drag up all the past" I stepped in and said, "all due respect but it's not the past when my mum is still having to live with it." My mum said again. "I want the permission needed of the sisters in which I asked for." Her face turned sour, her eye contact at this point was completely lost, she said "I remember the night they took you from the laundry car park, the fuss Angela made it's something I'll never forget. I'll speak with the others in the order and write back to you."

Myself and my mum left the care home elevated, we went to a local Irish pub next to O' Connell bridge, we laughed, talked and then took a stroll down the river, while talking my mum was talking about everything, everything she had missed all over the years. While walking we saw a caravan and she couldn't help but talk about what they took from her, her ma, her pa and sisters, the life they lived and the shame she carried for her ethnicity, we kept walking and talking as I told her that being a Irish Traveller is part of you that was one thing they couldn't actually take as it's in your blood, I told her not to let them and to be proud of all she was because myself and brothers was so proud of her, we kept strolling as in the distance the sun set on Dublin.

Once back in London. My mum then approached cork council where she made an application of exhumation, on the 8th October 2014 they replied.

It said:

"I acknowledge your receipt of your application in the above matter date 28 September 2014, we can identify the location of the remains of one Angela Collins, date of death 27/01/1988 at Section E, Row 12, Plot 5 in St. Finbarr's cemetery. Please submit the death certificate for your late mother to allow us to determine if that is the correct burial.

With regards to costs, cork city council charges £1,810.00 for carrying the exhumation and the cost must be paid in advance. You would also have to purchase an outsize coffin in which to seal the remains in and undertake the transport of the remains to their final interment in according with the terms set down by exhumation license. This usually entails transport by hearse. You would have to satisfy us that you have a cemetery plot in which to re-inter or have made suitable arrangements for cremation.

We also require confirmation that you are the nearest relative of the late Angela Collins, if there is a spouse, a parent, or other children of late Angela Collins still living they would also have to give their consent to exhumation. You might please confirm.

Lastly, we cannot make any alterations to the grave without consent of the owners of right of burial. I note on your application you say you have had no reply on this matter from the sisters of charity who own right of burial. I'm afraid of consent is not forthcoming, we cannot take any further steps in this matter. You may, if you wish, request the sisters to contact myself to answer any questions they may have."

She went back to the order and asked again, from here on, me and mother had approached the order face to face, via email and letter, with never any luck. After years slipping by my mum was giving up, I couldn't let that happen, I went to the funded group in my ignorance and asked for their help, they were very dismissive, I was just a young girl but I wasn't stupid but they treated me as such, I was never rude, I just wanted them to help push for the full outcome and couldn't understand their mentality when they were evasive and was saying it's all been dealt with.

I was too young and ignorant at that point to understand their behavior but I found out for myself even with being the nicest you can be, some people are put out there for a reason, they set out to not help and these people, they didn't wish to help my family just like the government didn't, they just wished to promote the governments agenda and will try crush anyone in their path who tried to disturb that.

I had nowhere else to turn and everywhere I did, I found no one wanted to help me and my mum, but I was going to prove them all that even as an uneducated looked down on traveller who just wants what's right as I've seen how it's effected my mum so badly throughout the years, instead of what the government wants and benefiting from, I was determined to expose the truth and the corrupt systems. So I decided what they will not do for those like my mum and family like they claimed to, I had to do so myself, I had to expose the truth as they was writing it in the way the government wanted it to be written instead of exposing the full truth regarding the institutions and their mass grave sites and the full history behind it for what it all really was, I told myself I cannot see my mum leave this earth without her seeing the truth being exposed, and seeing right being finally done by her after how much she has invested in gaining justice and trying expose the full truth for all involved.

I started off small, on 20th April 2015 I launched *Justice 4 All Magdalene Women & Children*, to the public, I was determined to make it a space where the cover up could be fully exposed, and justice pushed for all those effected.

During this time, a mother and baby home commission was set up and named fourteen mother and baby homes and four county homes. Although county homes were for the poorer in society and came with worse conditions than mother and baby homes, they were once the workhouses just renamed but they are not investigating them all as well as all the mother and baby homes run by orders in which had already been mentioned in past commissions in connection with abuse.

My mum and myself then planned that we was going to hold a protest out the Dáil in Dublin, I made all the posters and banners and marketed it to the best I possibly could, I was communicating with new and old members of the survivor community, Tuam had just broken to the public although it was something in which was mentioned during the Mcayleese report and was always known regarding further back from this point when bones was uncovered by young boys playing, but they covered back over it and said a prayer, but further research was out to support it at this time. There was many was calling it a hoax, but due to past commissions, the history and the accounts of my mum I knew it wasn't and supported it all the way, for this reasoning I had many attack me for standing by the theory of Catherine Corless, until it was confirmed by the commission there is in fact 800 babies in an out of usage sewage tank laying in Tuam.

Chapter 8.

Corruption Continues

Through beginning my organisation I met a lovely survivor called David, he wanted to help anyway he could with the protest which was for all interlinked institutions, we were pushing for finally a full investigation not just into the institutions and mass graves but the cover up around it.

Through my friend, David I became friends with a man who I'm going to refer to as JP. JP was so slick with the media, he had connections within it, he had already been on government panels, it claimed he was a private case in a mother and baby home where he stayed for 18 days before being adopted to a well-off family.

Before our first protest happened, I couldn't help myself and reached out to the government lead organisation for the Magdalene women & their families again, I needed to see if they would issue their support after trying to exclude my mum from the apology. When I got a response, I was happy to see they said they would attend. Within this protest, I was going to include the women medical cards as they were not provided special ones. On the day of that protest I couldn't see the organisation I invited present, I was gutted but went on with the day. However, I was happy to see a The Traveller's Voice came out to support us and also a man called Martin ward from tuam my mum was put in touch with. Martin in hopes he could help her find her fathers family. We stood with Martin on the day with my eldest daughter and had our pictures taken together.

After the protest ended, we went into Bushwells hotel for a drink, the founder of the organisation and others was sitting in there, she came over to say hi to us all and I just stayed away in the corner with my baby thinking if I went anywhere near her I would be honest in regards to her spending her funding money on food in a hotel yet they couldn't stand with us outside, it further confirmed to me they just don't care, I don't know why

I ever believed they would after being the ones to accept the brown envelope in regards to the laundries and being those who accepted to excluding people from justice, but after it being such a nice day, I wasn't going to say anything in which may have ruined it for my mum, no matter how much I really wanted to. But it just confirmed we was completely alone in this.

After our first protest in 16 July 2015 was a success, me and mum wanted to fly back over from London to welcome back the Irish government from their summer holiday. So, on the 22nd of September 2015, we returned to push the message for justice for all, again I got to work making all the posters, marketed the protest to the best of my ability and sent out press releases.

The morning of the protest we are waiting for a cab and I see a press release in which was published in the paper regarding the protest, JP claimed to the media my protest was his. He had previously written about me and my mums' story to the media and was putting his name, comment and group name with it, I did feel uncomfortable by this, but I just believed he wanted to help. Someone had warned me he was dangerous, but I was one of those people that I needed to see for myself and I was about to.

During the second protest In September we got out of the cab outside the Dáil with my mum, partner, brother and my baby in a pram, I had a banner and letter I wrote on behalf of everyone to walk down and hand into the justice department, as we jumped out of the car, a Garda started to shout, "across the road, behind the gates," I was interested to find out as to what had changed from the last time we were here, so asked why.

As soon as I spoke with my thick London accent, he looked at me as if I was filth. With his large figure towering over me, I pushed past my feelings of intimidation and I asked politely the reasoning as to why we couldn't stand on a public walk road, he further shouted at me, "now you listen to what I say to you women, get across the road"

I took a deep breath and while shaking, palms sweating, as he approached closer to my face, Worried I took out my phone but I wasn't about to back down as I knew my rights, so I asked again, "but why is that" and as I turned my back begin to walk across the road, he pushed me. I caught it all on camera, I turned around and ask, "why are you pushing me, is that not offensive?"

I continued speaking calmly with volume while shaking and distressed I said, "he just pushed me across the road all I said is I would like to stand here and excise my rights as my nan didn't have those rights, your government took my nan and put her in a Magdalene laundry."

I then witnessed him touch my mums back while guiding her across the road, I wanted to get the officers id regarding the assault and he said if I came back across the road I would be taken to the station in a paddy van, I wasn't about to create any further unnecessary upset or scare for my mum, so I stood down.

We then walked the letter down to the department and as we approached the doors of the department, the shutters came slamming down, my friend David had been into the department previously to inform them we would peacefully be handing in a letter, instead we were left outside, and the Garda was called. We explained everything and handed him our letter to give, I looked around at the faces of those in my community, my mums, my brothers and daughters and felt anger, feelings that cannot be explained in words, I felt sick knowing the feelings of rejection my mother was experiencing. After this occasion, my mum said she just felt like just jumping of the bridge, the effects they still continue to create through their extensive cover up and treatment of survivors. We felt truly gutted but returned to London to lick our wounds.

The survivor community was strong at this time, were all chanting the same message that we wanted a full investigation into all these interlinked institutions and mass graves and the cover up around it and most importantly supporting each other, well that was the genuine people effected by their crimes.

The mother and baby home commission was established and they named fourteen mother and baby homes and four county homes, the community was in outrage regarding this, they didn't want any more exclusive commissions in place that didn't result in all being investigated and no prosecutions for any criminal activity that took place, I was calling out Catherine Zappone and she put me as part of the commissions thread of emails, in hopes this would appease me, I kept speaking my mind and the truth publicly and was later removed of their commission thread, excluding me by not giving me any further information into their steps.

A survivor David had an idea for survivor group in which JP was more than up for it. JP, he took leadership, sent out all the emails of information and stated it's not to be a support group but a registered charity. They asked me to be a member of the panel being a daughter of a survivor and a big voice in the community but in the group's name it's states it's for survivors, I felt It wasn't that unless people are given a choice for it to be mixed, so I said I didn't wish to be part of the panel but I would love to help to see it make a difference.

Those in the community was campaigning for all to be included into the mother and baby home commission. There was discussions and distress from those in the survivor community of the extending the commission and JP told everyone to accept the terms and conditions and move on. Many people at this time started questioning themselves as to why he was so accepting to the governments exclusive agenda, while fully knowing that mother and baby homes in which was run by the same orders named in the Ryan report was excluded, which from my research it's over 300 county and mother and baby that had been excluded, at this point I was feeling so wary of JP but didn't show it yet. Until one day, he demanded that TDS be part of the panel and it be a mixed panel, I put back an email to JP and said how maybe a vote should be held for all survivors to decide, I wasn't going to let anyone use any survivor like my mum on my watch. After my mum being used by so many over the decades, I saw the signs and at this point this was my test to confirm it, if he is genuine he would allow a vote to be held, instead he became very defensive and manipulative and nasty, the same way in which previous government lead organisations for the Magdalene laundry's behaved when I said all needed to be acknowledged.

His friend who they were so close during the time of our protest, they stood together, whispered in each other's ears, that me and my mum believed and had mistaken them to be married, we only later found out they worked together to plant seeds in a community to have it torn apart and to break genuine people seeking full accountability for all crimes committed.

When I noticed there was no negotiation, I did my own survey regarding the vote, I just asked if a vote should be held and it came back that it should, after I took this action his friend who I'll refer to as MC shot back an email to me and told me I was manic and taunted me regarding mental health, although she is a qualified counsellor. These people together in their games had also caused a survivor in the community to have a stroke from all stress that they were put through after them targeting him, they also nearly made another survivor commit suicide by using the survivor's history against her.

Mum and I was so upset but we would never drop to a lower level to hurt another, we moved on from this, but the harassment didn't stop for me. Every move I made, they were there to attack, they got their friends to leave bad reviews on my organisation and personal page, every comment I made, they were there to not argue against my point but to call me a little girl who knows nothing regarding Ireland, who hasn't been effected by the institutions, when my nan lays in a mass grave and I've had to grow up watching my mum's sadness and how this cover up and the government has torn her apart. My nan could still be with us if she was given the treatment she needed and with 3 children now I see more all I missed out on from having my grandparents taken, they tried to cleanse me of my community by skipping a generation or two of the travelling people way, I have also been affected, just how can it ever be acknowledged when they will not even acknowledge our parents!

During this time they called me a bad mother when only after meeting me twice, they attacked me at every angle they possibly could, I was taking so many emotional blows, I felt like a school child again feeling completely alone in the corner of the playground, while having a massive group around me while my pretty bows were pulled out my hair as they smashed my head against a water fountain, but this time it was emotional blows and honestly, I thought I was strong enough not to but I was feeling every one of them. I did what I always do and stayed nice mannered and continued with my journey for my mum, nan and those alike but it wasn't to end here no matter how far I stayed away.

Chapter 9.

Sour flowers

On the 27/01/2016, My mum held a service on her mother's Angelina Collins death date for all the Magdalene women who lay in St. Finbarrs mass grave.

As I had previously said, mum had contacted the council regarding removing her mother's remains and was told the land the plot is owned by the sisters, so she would have to obtain the permission from them. She had written endless letters at this time which had been ignored.

The mass grave site that is meant to be under the church's care has not been look after and is also ignored like the women's existence was to them & still are even within the after life as there is no maintenance in place for the mass grave sites.

My mum contacted the sisters of charity before the event in hopes that they would like to show some remorse for their actions and would like to help acknowledge every individual who lays within the mass grave. With help from the welcome house she sent a letter through the post, I also personally sent two emails through their website and got no response. I then went on Facebook and also sent another two through their Facebook page, not to our surprise but there was no response.

On the day of the service my mum and one of her friends, had approached the building where the nuns are on the land of the laundry. My mum asked again for them to acknowledge these women in any small way but this time she asked in person, she asked for a bunch of flowers to lay from them on their behalf as they didn't wish to attend.

They kept saying they knew nothing regarding it or nothing about the Magdalene women or regarding the fact the many different forms we took to contact them in advance regarding it.

My mum also contacted the religious order by phone three times in advance. My mum recorded this whole discussion between three different individuals on day.

When my mum approached the last lady, she spoked with, she said we have no flowers, my mum said there are some there! The lady replies with "I would be killed if I dug them up"

In an environment where women were abused & drugged, a place where the nuns now use to accommodate their needs and after my mum explaining her mother's abuse in the laundry to her, on even the grounds they stood on. This we felt is not just a tongue and cheek statement. She spoke clearly throughout and then whispered it, you can hear it, but you need to listen closely to my mums recording. Why would she feel as if it was a secret, why did she lower her tone for others not to hear. This really is the question? Which is simply answered for us. Look at the history. Look at what they did to these women on these grounds and look at the lack of remorse! They haven't learned!

As they certainly do not care, they don't care about the seventy-two women that lay in the mass grave, within the land that they own, and they have no plan and never did to keep it maintained! They don't care that these women suffered wrongly and there is no acknowledgment of who they were!

They weren't the fallen Magdalene women, they were strong mothers, sisters, aunts, who was targeted for being a woman or from being in a community in which they wished to cleanse. The dead women should be acknowledge & these sites need to be treated with respect and as a part of Irish history! Yes, it's a shameful part of it but it's part of it! The history the church printed on Ireland along with the state, like they ignored and forgot these women they are now trying to ignore the mass graves they own and their duty to remember these women!

St Vincent's mass grave should be a historical site along with the other Magdalene mass graves throughout Ireland after being fully investigated. Instead it's a big neglected cross with a list of female's names on. It doesn't acknowledge the life's they were made to live, it is a shameful, disgusting part of Ireland history, but it is history! And it needs to be respected!

Even more so when there are living victims like my mum who was having to feel forced to visit a neglected grave that brings back memories of the abuse, she suffered from ages 2-18. Is it not time to start respecting these women and their families suffering? They ignore the request for my mum to remove my nan from the neglect mass grave without even a plaque to acknowledge who these women were. In the grave yard my nan is buried in St. Finbarr's cork, there are three unmarked mass graves of children. With nothing to mark their existence.

They ignored our attempt to try build a relationship with the religious order, they ignored their chance to try to rekindle the faith in their service. As once a catholic I was I taught to repent for my sins, so why didn't those who taught me those lessons, not practice them on the 27/01/2017 when they were given the opportunity to on many occasions by the victims & their families. I've also written two the pope twice and received no response.

Chapter 10.

Neglected Women

I was working hard keeping my head down doing all I could do to bring awareness to my mothers and nan's case, I had written to media outlets and had articles published and went on radio to extend the message regardless of my awful nerves, I was researching all aspects in which I could and what I would find would support my mums theory while growing up, that a high majority of women and children in these mass graves are from the travelling community.

I was also trying everything in power to bring awareness to the fact, the cover up is bigger than people really know or understand. I was informing that public that although they closed the Magdalene laundries in 1996 and the apology was issued in 2013, Magdalene women was still in the same dorms on the same land and in the same building of the Magdalene laundry. It was still also being run by the order who run the laundry the religious sisters of charity, many of these women was there with my nan and knew my mum as a young girl, who would be brought up to the laundries at the age of seven. All the women who would turn up at Angela's door in the laundry with the sweets they were all was treated with on a Sunday to give to the child that brought brightness to a very dark place.

The Magdalene women was made to stay on the same land run by the same people right up until 2017, reports were made by the hiqa report looking into what was now named St Vincent's centre for those with "intellectual disabilities" in the report, they found women's finances were being controlled, there was risk of fire and allegations of abuse which was not dealt with correctly.

The order although they still own the building handed it over to HSE for the running of the centre as standards was so low, they had a month to up standards and they failed the women and the future of the centre insuring the women who have been with each other for years and see each other as family live out the rest of their life's together, they started shipping the women out and separating them to different residences, some independent accommodations which made them use their payment of wages in 2013 for the process.

My mum and myself then set out to find out what would be happening to the building where my nan stayed for twenty-seven years and was neglected to death within. There were rumors of it being sold to a company in which they will build over everything and build housing, a journalist got in contact with me for more information as she was intending to approach the order to find out the future of the site. It was said by the order that they would be donating the building for housing, it will not be built over they claimed.

Those in our community believes that buildings such as Saint Vincent's which is in such good condition should be donated back to the community for education purposes such as setting up a museum to educate those within the community and those with parents, grandparents, effected by the institutions forever have a place in which they could be close to those they had taken and so the history is actually learnt from, which hasn't been the case within Ireland.

Chapter 11.

Ireland Never Learns

I was in correspondence with the justice department, I was trying to get them to take action for my mum and nan, although I sent them the response letter from cork council in the emails many times, they spoke with the order and they said they claimed we didn't make an application to the council. Although the order has responded to the justice department and two journalists, they have never responded in letter to us. But when the justice department said we didn't make an application after sending it to them, it proved that even then they would take their word as soiled gold while dismissing your evidence. I had sent an email straight back and stated they already had the evidence of them confirming they are lying but I provided them with the evidence again anyway in the council's application response letter.

The justice department responded with, as the letter states "it's between you, the order and your family, follow the steps set out in the response letter they and contact the religious sisters again" they replied sharply, I did so and again, we got no response.

I was desperate for some progress, then one day, I was shaken to read an article that the sisters of charity was the ones making progress, it was reported they would be given a hospital by the state. Outraged I couldn't hold in my emotions, I recorded a video to put online exposing all, I was saying that the sisters of charity, they was those whom had murdered my nan as the Catholic Church didn't believe in sterilization as is why she didn't get the treatment because of the catholic ethos, when she was recommended the hysterectomy, she didn't even have cancer, it was just making her very ill. During the decade they left her without, she developed cancer and they then dumped her body in a neglected mass grave!

I was determined to expose the order for what they had done and continued to campaign online, I went on the Joe Duffy show twice regarding the matter and them being given a hospital, it completely blew out. People took to the streets of Ireland with banners in hand, demanding this religious order not to be given a hospital, I felt proud in my country but not much was to change. The sisters of charity have tried to get around this by creating a charity called St Vincent's, they say they are not related although they constructed the charity and have shares within it, this matter is still ongoing in regards the people wanting a state-owned hospital, but it shows Ireland hasn't changed much.

So much so that the 27th January 2018 is another day I will never forget. The shame I felt towards my small hometown Ireland. I'm not sure it will now ever be wiped away while I see it has not changed, it was the day we held a remembrance event for my nan and all lives lost on the date of my nan's death.

But let's go back a little, a year previous from this day, my mother attended for the first time in years since being a young woman. She walked in the then renamed St Vincent's centre and a beautiful lady had stopped my mother while she was in the centre. With excitement, she said "I know you" she remembered my mum as a little girl aged seven who would visit the laundry to see her mum Angela, this was how I was to expose to the public, nothing change it's always a show for public while hiding the full extent, they just kept the women there, run by the same order and she wasn't the only woman who knew my mum there. But when she saw my mum again, she had so many precious stories to share with my mum Mary. They had a bond that was unbreakable and during our recent visit to see her it showed so much. This woman would save her Sunday sweets that all the women would get in the laundry on a Sunday and give it to Angela for when Mary her young daughter would arrive.

Seeing them part on the Saturday of 27th in the pub after the event was heartbreaking to watch. She said to my mum "you will come back to see me soon promise me". My mum replied, "I will come up on Monday before my flight back" the lady thanked my mother and my mum relied "I will never let you down"

The night before this lady had been taken out by the home to the opera house in cork, she explained to another woman on the day how many pictures she had with red Hurley whom was preforming there, keep this in mind for later as it's important. At the event, this lovely lady stood towards the grave with my mother. People started taking pictures and her care worker started calling her name and was saying "no pictures." The last year from this when this lady attended the event with my mum pictures was not a problem but sadly the following year, it was completely different.

I questioned why she could not have a picture and the lady's response was "it's our policy" I then said but what does she want? I looked towards the lovely lady standing next to my mum and wanted to give her a choice, it's her human right, she maybe older than us but not incapable of making her own mind up.

I said to her, "would you like to come down here and stand with me or have a picture?" She made it very clear where she wanted to be and that was next to my mum and next to another lovely survivor's side. She spoke clearly, "I want to have a picture a taken" this day was so important to her and she had every right to be there and fully take part and she had made it very clear she had wished to.

Not in a million years was I going to pull her of the grave step and say, "no your carer has said you don't deserve that right, you don't deserve to be treated as an equal to the other survivors here as" I was going to stand by what I know is right.

This woman entered the laundry aged eighteen, she spent her whole life in that laundry and has some amazing knitting skills, her whole life she was restricted simple human rights, my nan was restricted a hysterectomy for over a decade while there and never was I going to stand against someone's right to choose! I felt the upset for my nan and saw nothing had changed. I turned to the carer and said, "well you heard her." The care worker than began to cry. I asked why? She first said because she felt bad that the women couldn't be properly part of the day, but she has to call someone down here and then she walked away from the group.

She got on her phone and called another woman to the grave yard via cab. She then stopped us on our way out to try to again explain why we cannot take pictures. She explained it's a policy. I simply said, "can I have a copy of that policy". After stuttering for an excuse, she then said, "it's confidential." The other lady said "I wouldn't even be able to take pictures of her and I work with her. "

Let's think back to the opera house I mentioned earlier which the wonderful lady deserved, which took place just the night before the event. What happened? Aw yes. Pictures was taken! So basically, it proved because it was with survivors and their families and it showed this woman is still on the same land, she was enslaved on with the women she knows to be in that mass grave so it wasn't acceptable to them. That's what I was getting from it all. They don't want the truth to be known by the public.

Before attending the event as we waited to take the lady out of the home, we waited for the carer to get her coat. The lady who knew my nan had stated very clearly "I'm not trusted to go alone" my heart sank, little did I know it was about to sink even further once we got to the grave site.

I said to the second carer, "your saying it's policy so why when my mum attended last year was it okay for her to have lots of pictures." In my mind, I was thinking they must know people have been educating others regarding how Magdalene women stayed under the care of the religious order right up to 2017 and they don't want any more exposure. She then stated because we have been taken over. I fired back "I'm aware of that, HSE correct. But still you cannot produce a policy?" Then later in the pub the lady stated about red Hurley the night before so clearly there was no such policy. It was just a policy they made for this woman for that day. To benefit just them.

After the first carer stating she started crying due to the women's lack of rights "not being able to take part fully in the day" she tried to later say she began to cry as people was screaming and shouting at her. I made clear that was a lie. People was just voicing it was so wrong. No one even raised their voice while doing so. It was a respectful event and remained that way regardless of the intrusion.

She then tried to say, "it was the American man who shouted". There wasn't an American man present, he was in fact Irish and was in a mother and baby home and he was just passionate in the way he speaks and was one to speak up. Another brave lady stepped in and said, "he did not shout" and then the carer claimed it was due to the group size and she felt intimidated. I stated that's fair enough and was understandable, but no one shouted but down the phone to her colleagues she had clearly stated that from the start because as we looked up the path, a third women was walking down with a furious face, all three was out for one little lady. "It was like the matron mother whom was walking down to tie a situation up for nuns struggling to do her dirty deeds" my mum said after. The other carer did try to listen and discuss things and I would honestly say came across nice apart from the change of story from what she stated to me the reason she began to cry.

This third woman was however harsh. She would shut people down and not listen. She said they will not have their staff upset. But will see the lady they care for by restricting her right and didn't listen to her feeling upset that she is not equal to others. She tried to state the day before when my mum came to visit, she hadn't even asked about the event taking place. Just it was a visit and they knew nothing regarding an event until the morning we turned up. Another lie!

I said they that's not true, why would they ask us to call them back regarding it then after 3:30 as a funeral was taking place on the day we attended so we couldn't see my mums friend. I said I even have the phone call on my phone and reached for my bag to get it and she said, "save it I don't care we know how to do our jobs" very aggressively, no one could speak to this woman unless you agreed with everything she said and I wasn't going to while she told lies.

So regardless I got up the number up and at 1:25 on the Friday before the event after our visit, we called as we were requested to do. It was the day before the event and we were told to call back after half three, the call was made at four and they told us to attend in the morning before the event.

We then took the lady who knew my nan in the Magdalene laundry down to the pub after the event. We all sat around with three carers paid for by the state for one woman. Like two cabs was paid for by them to all wastefully attend. It was like she was a prisoner silenced by their presence. It was what I call sadly a disgrace on their behalf and the country who let this all continue as they never called for a full inclusive investigation into every aspect of these homes and the cover up.

The carers made me feel uncomfortable so I left the pub six months pregnant and I walked back down to the grave with my partner Billy and my youngest daughter at the time Amelia to clean the rubbish around the grave as I didn't feel I got to do what we really wanted to do due to this horrible demonstration of control and I went back just to genuinely reflect on the circumstance.

Once back in the pub I took my eldest daughter Angel into the toilet and while the lady and one carer pushed the door to come in I heard her say "when are you wanting to leave?" She stopped the discussion when she saw me and complimented my dress and explained how she hated being out in these environments while not dressed up, I told her that she looked nice regardless but she said, "it's okay for in the centre but these places no way" I laughed it off and walked out and sat down.

After that she walked back in with the lady from the toilet and she took her place back where she was seated next to my mum, the carers then took some minutes to whisper something to each other and then announced how the lady sitting next to my mum said she wants to go now, they said "she needs to have her nap".

We all got up and said goodbye to the lovely lady and that was when she and my mum had that heartbreaking conversation; she didn't even finish her drink before she had got up off her seat. She downed the last little bit of her drink while standing, some cheered her on. She looked up with a big cheeky smile and left the pub followed by her three carers, all there for one tiny, slow walking figure. I then went to take a seat next to my mum who looked deflated. I took the lady's space and looked down to notice she hadn't even finished half of her soup they ordered for her.

Another woman in the group said that when the lady came back from the toilet, she had heard her say to her she had to go now, and the woman replied by asking if she had wanted to. She said her reply was "no". I felt broken. While she told me this, this lovely lady became so emotional, she was brought to tears bless her, as told me this.

While walking away from the pub with my mum. I stated to her it hadn't changed, just adapted and we all felt like complete rubbish. We can't stop people from taking pictures with their family or friends or like the lady wanted a picture the night before at the opera house with red Hurley when it was granted, they should not have restricted, humiliated her the way they did on the day. Last year there wasn't any noticeable cameras on the Magdalene laundry site which was turned into the care Centre, but the dorms are where the women would have been, and the church at the back is all closed down with stickers of "cctv in operation around which was once never there.

The convent where the sisters of charity live is literally next door on the same spot of land as this laundry and is newly built, they moved out from the laundry into there, those in the centre and the sisters of charity Covent are all behind one big high wall but the sisters they have a little wall and gate surrounding their convent named St. Anthony's and last year the gates to the convent was open for my mum to enter but this year on both occasions we visited, the gates were closed.

My mum attended the place her mother was locked up in for twenty-seven years and when she was spotted by this beautiful woman who worked beside my nan. Since then everything has changed, she stated. They have tightened up the security for the centre.

My mum said while walking back that the lady had said last year how she would love to visit London where my mum lives and she promised it to her. Holding back her tears she said "but look at them, look at the way they treated her, they would never let her have that freedom. She cannot even leave without a carer although such a strong, capable woman. I would look after her so well during her time over, but I know even if we both begged they would never let her, she deserves the dignity and respect they never gave and to deny her the right to remember her friends in peace like we did together the previous year and they didn't listen to her voice or what she wants, they never did for these women nor their children and didn't do that on that today, it's all made us feel both sick.

Broken, hurt and angry to see nothing had changed, we got on the bus and went back to our hotel room. Ireland and its institutions hadn't changed much and had just continued to cover up and the reason they wish for no pictures of these women and don't leave them alone is because it uncovers the big blanket, they have all covered over it all. No one in a position to help me and my mum, would.

Although the day on my nan's death date for all lives lost was high jacked by an emotional, passive aggressive team paid for by the Irish state, we have come away with more knowledge and education as shameful and sickening as it all is. We learned it's so hard to get justice in Ireland as they are still restricting rights of living humans who they made slave away for the state and church and there is a massive cover up behind it all. They closed the laundry, then kept them hidden in the same building, on the same land, ran by the exact same people. The Irish government they left the women under their care of those who said they will not contribute a penny to the Magdalene women's wages. Those who Caranua were paying 100k of survivor's money to provide counselling services to those children they abused, they should have done it for free or not at all considering its a bias service by those who committed the actions and is just inconsiderate to the survivors who may have anxieties towards the institutions who abused them.

The sisters of charity owned the laundry site right up till the year 2017 and when more awareness was spread regarding ownership and the standards was found to be falling, it was then reported to have been handed over to HSE where they didn't even up standards in the time frame set. At my Nan's remembrance event, it showed on the day not much has changed so no wonder they all happily continue to ignore my nan's right to a single resting site and the sisters of charity do not maintain and respect the site they own.

Chapter 12.

Travelling People Buried There

Things didn't calm down with the government cronies as much as I ignored them, they made lies up regarding not just me but many against those in the community that they couldn't ever back up with evidence, JP and his friend MC used not only past criminal records to hush survivors in the community but also women's past, while they was becoming part of Katherine Zappones panel for the mother and baby home commission and being both those who was selected for the secret meeting with pope Francis when he attended Ireland in August 2017, where he claimed to know nothing in regards to the Magdalene laundry's. No one was told when or even if this meeting was to be taking place and those two again was the ones chosen together, while being those who tore shreds into others and into the full action and for all mentally. A survivor was on the verge of suicide at this time, she left the mother and baby home and sadly was picked up by a controlling pimp, when JP used her history to try silence her, she denied it, which she lately proudly came out strong regarding to the press about. She had nothing to be ashamed of, many who left institutions became further abused by another in some way like sadly my mum did by my dad. It was JP who ought to be ashamed, they were dragging all genuine people through the dirt, using foul language and untruthful statements, bullying in whatever manner they possibly could, it got so serious the Garda got involved in some cases. I was already pushed on the sidelines as after my nan's event, they put me in a total state of depression while heavily pregnant, they slandered me to the last degree which they could not prove with any evidence, but through it all I never gave up, they would knock me down again and again but I kept coming back to speak of my nan, mum and those alike and regarding the cover up publicly.

I started focusing on all the Irish government had missed and excluded and researched every aspect I could, I wasn't going to let their cronies achieve their goal of distraction. I started asking myself questions regarding my nan's mass grave and things that didn't add up and with my mum's accounts in my solitude. They weren't exposing the truth, so I made sure I was to set out to get it, so while they tried to tear the community apart, played dirty tricks, the old divide and conquer technic. I couldn't lose focus, as that's exactly what they wanted. I was alone but I had my mums support, I kept on track and their bullying help me to do that.

Back in the March 2017, through my research I revealed 1/3 of the babies in Tuam could be from the travelling community and showed that 65% of the whole community during the time could have been targeted in Tuam and put in the septic tank, it was published in the Irish Sunday & Sunday mirror.

Moving on from this looking through the names recorded via a funded research group, I was frustrated when I saw the Magdalene names project only recorded three mass graves in relation to three Magdalene laundries out of twelve totaling to 487 bodies.

The research group had recently updated the site and they no longer go to mass graves to hand record the names, instead they get records of data from how many was in the laundries and from the electoral register, which doesn't show how many of these women died, so it didn't really help with my research but going through the census I noticed although my nan was in St. Vincent's Magdalene laundry for 27 years, she lays in a mass grave owned by the sisters of charity, she was not even recorded to be present in the laundry.

Therefore, you cannot even trust data, even the headstones are untrustworthy, some women may have been left unrecorded but it's the only thing I had to work with, so with the very little of the three separate sites of recorded names I had, I further went head.

By using the list of surnames, I used in my previous research in 2017 I could go through the names and by hand, spot the surname in relation. Then number and write out the name and surname of the person.

By using my old method, I was able to reveal that:

High park Magdalene laundry, Dublin.

At High park, it has 174 women names recorded on the stone. 105 traveller surnames was recorded to be part of the figure of 174.

Using my previous research, I was able to see if any of the 105 traveller surnames had any connection to the site in Tuam, 60 traveller surnames was the same as some of the babies in Tuam. Further showing partial families for generations was targeted.

At high park the research determines that 60.344% of Travellers could be buried there.

St. Vincent's Magdalene laundry, cork.

For St Vincent's on the headstone 72 women are recorded.

36 of those names buried in St. Vincent's plot showed to be Irish Traveller surnames.

At St. Vincent's I found Irish Traveller surnames connected to Tuam mass grave, was 24 Travellers surnames.

The research shows at St. Vincent's 50% of Irish Travellers could be buried at the site.

Good shepherds Magdalene laundry.

Limerick had 241 names recorded on the grave stone.

170 of the surnames buried in the plot showed to be traveller surnames.

72 shows to be the same as those babies buried in Tuam.

The research shows at the good shepherds 70.539% of Irish Travellers could be buried at that mass grave site.

Only one family out of the 487 names recorded in three separate Magdalene mass grave sites have come forward to identify one woman. That family is ours. Why out of such a large number of people dead, has only one family come forward? I wanted to find this out so did some more research.

Irish Travellers have been excluded from the history books and even government policy's such as the poor act. We can only assume when looking at figures regarding Irish

Traveller's like I have with only the surnames to go by to try determining how many in our community was targeted.

Although the first commission of inquiry into the poor laws In Ireland made no references to "itinerants" etc. it was clear that matters concerning the travelling people were of central importance to the proceedings. The latter of the body was concerned with the burden on maintaining "foreign" paupers and demanded introduction of settlement laws in Ireland so that ether the mobile poor could be returned to where they came from or the cost of the relief could be recovered by the ratepayer in the pauper's origin.

Given the concern with wandering poor the commissions research into the populations inhabiting the workhouses revealed an unexpected absence. Missing from the disorderly contents of the mixed workhouse was a figure long known to use it as shelter of last resort.

Research carried out by the commission found casuals were occasionally being received in county homes, (the new name for work houses) but the number seeking admission was so low that it raised question as to what might be happening to this class. Stating "that although this class is not recorded, we know they exist" the Garda was requested to conduct a census of "homeless persons observed wandering on highways in single night in November 1926" the result of the census is reported in the table below. As you can see inside the metropolitan area was very low, while those outside the metropolitan area is very high.

It's not possible to discern from this information the extent to which itinerants are enumerated among the general population of "homeless persons" although it's seems reasonable to assume that they are likely to have been counted among classes 3 and 5, which together amounts for 64 percent in total.

The fact that the large amount of people is from the outer area also aligns with being the travelling people and the large numbers of women and children. Especially in category 3, would suggest we are looking at traveller families here rather than individuals.

This was before the commission of itinerancy, they were taken children from their family to make them efficient workers, so there was the supply there and to completely eradicate the travelling people. By using our reports, you can tell they was more concerned with the nature of the family such as they are living circumstances and ethnicity rather it being for the safety of their children. My research all together shows that they tried to commit a genocide of a small community all in which has been ignored.

Chapter 13.

Honour The Magdalene's

One morning mum saw an article regarding honouring the Magdalene's event, she was down that she hadn't been invited the morning me and my partner and children was staying over a night at her house, I said write an email mum, she goes, "Laura you know I'm not good at them things could you do it?"

I was more than happy to, we got a reply quickly from the justice department. Which advised us to the government funded Magdalene support group. I prepared an email for my mum in response and we got a reply from one of the founders, you already know the one, the one who turned up to our protest and sat in the hotel eating. In her response, she said to my mum can come to the second dinner but the first she will not be allowed, it's just for the living working residents in whom they acknowledged in the apology, not child residents or children of these women. But she responded with "relatives" fully knowing my mum was in the laundry as a child, as in the early days of their group, they spoke to and used my mums and nan's story for their site, so was fully aware she wasn't just a relative. However, the only condition was my mum would have to pay for her flights.

My mum was already aware by talking to other survivors in the UK, it's being funded by the justice department including flights, I prepared another email and stated we would just be contacting the justice department regarding the exclusion.

She quickly replied and told us not to do that, give her a little while and she can see what she can do. Indicating she was in the wrong. She came back and said my mum can have the flights covered but it just demonstrated again if you're not in their inner circle of following their agenda, they wrongly exclude you.

On the day, my mum flew over for the event, not only was family members at both the dinners but was also part of the bit in which was just for the living working residents. It's just my mum and some others weren't allowed in due to space, one lady even asked my mum "where's Laura?" on the day of the dinner, "you could have brought her along," further proving they purposely excluded my mum and her family. They tried to hand out jewelry to everyone but after being excluded from the full day my mum didn't wish to accept it. The whole event just didn't feel right for her, while those who was not even in institutions was part of the whole day such as the founder who has not been anyway affected after trying to exclude my mum. For my mum to be a baby resident and a seven-year-old child who had to visit, and they tried to exclude her, it felt empty and fake. They still hadn't acknowledged everything, and people were being looked after in hers and mums name whom had no relation. While survivors for a day were handed down scraps, cheers and empty gestures for the public to look on and think the government do a lot by those women, when justice is still being withheld.

How can people pretend to honour Magdalene's when they do not honour the graves they lay in and cover up on their manner of death? When the full history is covered up and they exclude all those they committed crimes against, while mass graves lay neglected, broken, unseen. We are honoring no lives lived by the Magdalene's, when they refuse to give simple rights to survivors and relatives for exhumation processes and leave them in neglected sites.

My mum came back very depressed from this event, you're not honoring the lives' when in 2013, they issued an apology in the Dáil and didn't say sorry to all those affected and all the lives' lost. Not even a minute's silence to our dead. That's how much Ireland honours our as they say "Magdalene's".

In 2003 the Irish times reported back in 1993, undertakers exhuming the bodies of 133 women at a Sisters of Our Lady of Charity convent found 22 others remains and almost 60 of the deaths at one of the infamous Magdalene Laundries in Dublin were never registered. The shocking revelations did prompt calls by the public for a Garda probe into who these women were, and how they died.

The Sisters of Our Lady of Charity sold off land at their High Park convent in Drumcondra, Dublin, to developers in 1993.Part of this land included a graveyard containing the remains of 133 women who had been locked away for years without pay in the laundry.

The Department of the Environment granted a license for the removal and cremation of the bodies at nearby Glasnevin cemetery but undertakers who began removing the coffins found an extra 22 remains. Many of the bodies were buried with their broken bones still in plaster-casts on their ankles, elbows,

wrists, and hands when they were taken out of the ground, one
of the bodies was headless.

It is said that when they found the bodies the department simply
issued an extra license covering the other remains and did not
launch an investigation into who they were.

Failing to register a death is a criminal offence but the
sisters and those above them were allowed to get away with no
criminal prosecutions, again. Of the 133 original bodies, just 75
death certificates existed, all 155 bodies were removed and all
but one of them was cremated which is odd as the Catholic
Church had frowned heavily upon that action.

The women now can never be identified in the event of
an investigation into their deaths as all the evidence has been
burned. The then Minister for Justice Michael McDowell, was
asked to initiate a criminal investigation into the unregistered
and unexplained deaths but a spokeswoman said:" That's a
matter for the gardai but there is no investigation into these

unexplained deaths at the moment." The Department of the Environment was reported as saying that "no trace" forms were issued for 34 of the dead women and it could not search for the identities of 24 others because of "insufficient details". In the case of the 34 women, the department added: "It appears that the statutory registration procedures were not complied with at the time of their deaths." Of the 22 extra bodies, it said it only had details of 14 of them.

The Sisters of Our Lady of Charity defended its actions. A spokesperson Sister Ann Marie Ryan said that the exhumation and re-interring of all 155 women were "approved by all relevant authorities we have had no queries from families about our decision in the intervening time. One family took the remains of a deceased relative to a family plot at the time. The remaining 154 were respectfully cremated and laid to rest at a public ceremony."

In 2018, the public was informed that the cemetery in which my nan is buried in a mass grave in, there are two unmarked graves containing children beside it. The last child buried there was in 1990. In the case of the last burial in 1990, the child's death certificate notes that while she died in St. Finbarr's Hospital in Cork, she was in the care of the nuns at Bessborough Mother and Baby Home. A birth entry for this child in this name could not be located.

I personally believe they fear opening the mass grave to my nan which is said to have seventy-two women in it and all other sites like it because they fear it will uncover another criminal circumstance and it will expose the full truth as to who these children and women in Tuam, cork etc. really are, it will answer why their families have not come forward as they purposely cut ties. So, they ignore us, but they cannot ignore Tuam any longer with public pressure as is why in 2019, the exhumation and DNA process will begin.

I have sent so many letters and emails to the government and religious orders, I even contacted TDS and the justice department but the sisters of charity, an organisation that have proven to break the law within burials in the past who were allowed to just get away with it! They are the ones to have the last say and control on this matter regarding my family.

Chapter 14.

DNA Doesn't Lie

For weeks, a little test had been sitting in my mother house that was sent from ancestry.com She was so nervous she left it there. For my mum Mary, this was understandable as in the industrial school she was told her family was murderers and thieves and she was beaten due to her mother. She was also told she would end up like them. She feared everything regarding her family. When her abuser made her bleed or she fell over and she looked at the blood she believed the blood was dirty blood, everything about herself and family she despised.

For weeks, I had been joking "have you done it yet mum, when you gonna spit in the bottle" it laid there until a day myself and mum met up. That morning without even me having to remind her like the weeks in advance, she suddenly gets the urge to use the kit that cost her a hundred odd quid and has been sitting in the box for weeks. She then left the house and met myself and daughter and asked for angel (my eldest daughter) to be the one who would send it off for her. I picked her up and she slipped in through the red post box.

The weeks following, we were nervous, would we even find anything worthwhile. Little did we know we was about to strike gold. I kept excitedly saying to mum "is it here yet?" And finally, my mum sends me an email and says check it and called me immediately after to discuss it. Together we looked through trying to work the site, she had 234 odd pages worth of cousins, 166 of just 1st- 4th cousins, the first message we constructed was to the highest relative.

Marion Rose, we discussed what to say to her, the nerves were already hitting us hard. What's the right thing to say? How do we go about something like this, we were thinking? We had chosen to provide names of her parents in hopes we would get a reply. We gave what information we had, and she replied fairly quickly, thankfully so we didn't have to sit on our hands for too long.

She had said regarding her mother named Bridget having a sister named Angela in Peacock Lane, Cork. Straight away we knew this was my nan. Marion Rose is my mother's first cousin. She provided everything she possibly could bless her kind heart, she even told us to get in contact with her son, who is such an intelligent, respectful, caring young man. Keiran. My mum is so proud to get to call them her relatives.

He is also in the care profession like my mother which my mum adores and she got so excited with the similarity. He was so emotional from learning regarding his great aunt Angelina.

To see my mother's & nan's beautiful caring family taken from my mum due to prejudice and the lack not being able to trace them due to the orders restricting information!

Why didn't the laundry who knew my mum was visiting there right up till her mum died. Why didn't they provide her with her aunts address which would of lead her to her cousins, aunts and uncles!

Angela's sister was writing to Angela in the laundry before her death, my mums' cousin still has these letters from Angela. Her friend Mary Ellen Moran was also in the same Magdalene institution, once Angela died, she would write to my mum's aunt and say how much she missed Angela. My cousins told us this. Bridget my mother's aunt died in 2015, they had her address and my mum had been visiting the laundry right up until Angela died! She was so ill my mum even went to see her GP while she was locked in the laundry! When she died why didn't the nuns give my mum this information. They kept family connections purposely away.

Why didn't they give my mother this address so she could reunite with some of her mother's family after losing her mother due to them not providing the lifesaving treatment recommended by the doctors. It was restricted for ten years for her to be left to work ill and then die. My mum had no one and they knew that, they knew the address of her aunt. As they would have been writing the letters on Angela's behalf as they claimed she was illiterate and later the address was to Mary Ellen Moran who wrote to inform my mums aunt her sister had died. Ellen Moran was my nan's friend and was the last name on the Magdalene mass grave in cork, she died 9/2/1992.

They purposely kept our lovely family away from us, Bridget died in 2015, my mum, brothers, and even my eldest daughter would have got to meet her if the church didn't stop us! Like they stopped us meeting my nan due to them taking her life! My nan died 5 years before I was born in 1988.

The emotions for my mum have been crazy, she cried when she saw pictures, she always believed her family was something to fear, when our cousin sent us a picture of my great nanny, her nan! My mum said:

"They could have placed me with her. Instead I was put in an industrial school from the age of 2 so they got a payment from the state and kept me in an abusive system when I had about ten aunts and uncles and a nan! But my aunt wasn't even aware of me"

My mum also said while looking at a picture of her nan:

"I would have been protected with her, she so beautiful, the beautiful beads, she is wearing little earrings and I love her coat. Wow, she looked so strong, she only died 5 years before Angelina did, I honestly feel so happy, I've gained insight and have such a welcoming, kind family but through it all, it's riddled with sadness as I lost out on being with my nan, my aunt but to know one day I will meet her lovely daughter makes my heart lift from that sadness. I will not stop though until I gain full justice for the clear actions they took to erase peoples' routes by not providing the information the church actually had and to think I was scared of such lovely people, it's the institutions, they beat it into me but like I've seen throughout the years they are liars! They are the thieves! They called me number five! And tried to take my identity & family away. They robbed me. Thank God for DNA! They had my aunts address! I could have met her way before she died, I'm hurt, and it makes me feel sick they did that to me. All the nuns knew me, I was that little girl that would visit the laundry from the age of 7 to visit my mum and from what I learned from reports recently I was also toddler living as a resident by them. I just don't understand how evil you have to be to do this to people, anger is not the word for my emotions but I'm also very happy."

We have all been invited down to the mum's aunts grave where she lays in the Leicester in UK to pay our respects at her grave with her cousins which we are so grateful and pleased to have had the offer! They couldn't be closer to perfect! They have already been so accommodating and provided us with all the information they know. Which we will forever be truly grateful for. The truth always comes out in the end and myself and mother and my bothers are so glad it has, and we will keep seeking for the rest of it.

Through using the DNA service, we were able to also connect with other cousins all other the world in America, Australia and the UK. It's been an amazing experience and has helped us piece everything further together even with the doctored records but along the way we have had some shocks.

My mum became friends with a woman called Margaret through an adoption group, together they stood against bullying in the group and became good friends. One day a notification email from ancestry site came through and told my mum regarding a new cousin having signed up, her name was Margaret Goodman, she had the same picture she had on her Facebook my mum was shocked. Margaret was an ancestry wiz and had very quickly connected her tree, she begins helping me with my mums. This was when it was confirmed Shayne wards mother Philomena Joyce is my mums double first cousin. Philomena's mother Margaret Collins was my nans Angelina's first cousin as was Philomena's father Martin Joyce which was my nans first cousin. All those years ago when we were in our little three-bedroom house snug on the sofa with a pack of chocolate mints watching him on telling, feeling the connection, it all became real. Irish Traveller's being cut of from society and for security would marry their cousins throughout generations making the children double cousins, giving a higher DNA rating than cousins who are not double relations. Double cousins have the same DNA equivalent as someone who is half siblings. But this confirmation with Margaret regarding Shayne was all just the beginning of our odd discovery's.

One morning we received a message viva the site from John Ward asking how we was related, I looked at his picture and expressed how he looked a lot like martin ward. In 2015 we attended a protest we arranged and took pictures with Martin ward who was once former mayor of tuam. I told my mum to ask him if he was related to him and he confirmed he was his brother. We were in total shock, we questioned ourselves as to how oddly the world works sometimes, we were walking among our cousins the whole time and we didn't know, strangely family relations brought us back together before DNA did, I began speaking with martins other siblings and his amazing educated daughters Lauren and Mariah, I was touched by the fact his daughter Mariah, who was soon to be wed, invited my mother and I to her wedding. They have truly welcomed us into the family with open arms. Lauren works on her own little business and has two beautiful children. Gerard their brother has also been very welcoming and has beautiful children of his own also. We went from having no cousins, to having a strong Irish family of many.

Chapter 15.

I Can't Pretend This Journey Is Over

We have just got through another Christmas remembering my nan and aunt who took her life, on that day, with my mum, brother Anthony, and my partner Billy and my three daughters Angel, Amelia and Anastasia. My brother Craig spent this year in America with his wife's family but will be over in the following year. My aunt Teresa said she would be with us this year for Christmas which would have been our first ever Christmas together, she said she would stay the night and booked train tickets but sadly, not to our surprise but to our disappointment she didn't show.

We will not be attending my nan's mass grave next year on the 27 January 2019 like we normally do as financially things are difficult currently, we are planning to with all my children and mum this coming summer when this book will be launched. During this journey, I was approached by a kind lawyer who wanted to try help regarding my nan. He said he would write a letter to the sisters of charity, he did so, and like us. Got no response.

My mum had contacted Garda and will be attending Ireland also soon to have a DNA test with all six of the children remains she believes could be her relatives. She strongly believes six children, have a very strong chance of being closely connected to her family. An if so, she wants to remove her relatives remains from Tuam.

My mum at the time said:

"The Garda in Tuam was very helpful to my request. They are waiting for direction for the commission currently and will be in touch soon. They have taken down my details for when they start doing DNA tests on the remains. I just hope they don't give me excuses as to why DNA tests can not take place in the near future, I asked if other people had come forward and he said slowly, one a day, which I'm so pleased to hear as it shows Ireland is not ashamed anymore."

My mum has reason to believe her unconfirmed relatives were neglected, as baby Geraldine Collins who died at thirteen months, had flu at three months and was marasmus, which means undernourishment causing a child's weight to be significantly low, this started at three months and she died just over a year old. So, although the Garda released a statement saying" if there is no crime, meaning there is no investigation". These children were in their care and were undernourished. That's neglect and can be punishable in a court of law.

The names of children, my mum believes to be part of her large travelling family that comes from Tuam.

1947
Geraldine Collins,13 months.
1934

Luke ward, 15 months.

1928

Joseph ward, 7 months,

1947

Thomas Collins, 17 months.

1937

Bridget Collins. 5 weeks.

1936

Eileen Collins. 2 months.

My mum will now never get justice regarding my mum's abuser Bernadette who they let escape to London to work in St. Guys hospital in London around more vulnerable people and then travelled to America to live out the rest of her life without consequences. She not only abused my mum but many other girls, a girl who reported the abuse to father Conner in cork was told to forgive and forget and to look out for her after her beating her and many children senseless, many people protected this woman.

We were only informed this year that the lady part of the sisters of mercy who abused my mum and others, died. She escaped without facing prosecution due to the protection of the state and church. Even though my mum also reported this woman to Garda and they said if she ever came back into the country that they would stop her at the airport and bring her in for questioning. When she came to visit Ireland, they didn't do what they said they would.

My mum made an official complaint to the Garda after the Ryan report failing to prosecute those involved within her and other children abuse. My mum and many other girls complained regarding this woman and her treatment, she worked in an industrial school in cork. She sexually, physically and mentally abused many girls.

The Ryan report had many young women come forward regarding her, but they had acted upon nothing! Regardless of telling the victims they intended to follow things up. This was in 90s when this all began and nothing had been done by them. The state, with also the protection of the church, let the women flee Ireland to London to start doing her training in St. Guys, hospital. London bridge. She was taught nursing there, and worked with more vulnerable adults, maybe again children! Who knows but once the Ryan report hit the headlines, she left St. Guys and fled to America!

When my mum made her report to the Garda it was over half a decade ago now, they said many other girls had also came forward and if she was to land in Ireland she would be arrested. But instead, she had been able to travel back into Ireland without arrest.

The Garda had lied to victims to protect the government and church, meaning they are not protecting the people nor their children of Ireland at the current time while they are letting these people, they know to be dangerous, among the public. The Gardaí have been pretending to correspond with America, when they had no intention of prosecuting her for the crimes she committed on the girls in the industrial school and bring her back from the very start. They had let her travel over to Ireland and walk the streets as a free woman. This nun was part of the vaccine processes on the children in the homes. She would pin them down while they injected their little bodies. She knew everything regarding the government involvement within the child abuse in the homes, as is why someone at the top was protecting her, like they are protecting other sexual & physical abusers of children, to protect themselves.

My mum has been speaking with the Garda at that point for six years. She had called him after getting many reports and sightings of this women in Cork, where the Gardaí station is meant to be dealing with the reports.

"They had not just let her enter Ireland, but the area they are based in. "My mum said to the Garda, and he said, "well maybe she could have, she is not on the terrorist list"

Which my mum sharply replied, "but you said if she hit an Irish airport, she would be arrested."

He stuttered, but his next thought was to say, "well maybe she traveled over with a fake passport"

My mum then said, "but you just said she is not on the terrorist list, so you weren't planning to arrest her in the first place."

His voice then deepens, and he says "Mary, you need to write to the justice department, and get a solicitor."

As he knew this case was being stopped and was not allowed to go anywhere. Because if the government prosecute the criminals within the church, they will expose the government and the larger part they played within these institutions for mothers & children then they really let on. It would also expose the Parma businesses for the part they played within the institutions. Although my mum went through all of this, she escaped facing prosecution as she died this year.

Tulsa has been caught for keeping child sexual abuse records stored away to collect dust, instead of being investigated. Out of 800 cases, they now plan to investigate 20. They are waiting for the criminals to die, so they both get away with it. 780 cases have been left to get away with, due to a clear cover up by the Irish government! They have sealed all abuse records for 75 years as then who will be left living who is affected to care.

My mum and family fly over to Dublin again, to make an official complaint to the garda regarding my nan's death. My mum is such a quirky character you can always expect some excitement with her, while flying from Stanstead airport we had all our tickets book my mum, previous to booking my mum said that she would book hers and my eldest daughters flight while I booked for myself, partner and at the time my youngest daughter. We got to the airport and the women had said the ticket name did not match with the name on the passport for my eldest daughter. Which was what my mum booked. We panicked. However thankfully it could be resolved but we had to pay £50 pound. It had put us right behind in regard to time. We rushed to where there was a massive que at security and said "that was it, the protest, the need to make a formal report, mum we are f****d we cannot let all those who are expecting us down" my mum looked at us all " where there is a will there is a way. Follow my lead". My mum then started saying out loud "I'm so sorry but our plane is at this time and we are not going to make it", the good will of the people helped us and they all pulled us to the front, the crowd was pushing our backs as my mum looked back with her cheeky smile while thanking the kind members of public . It never seemed to stop for us, the crazy journeys, the meetings, the vigils, the protests, while on the plane I was looking out the window, I thought back to year 2017 we were in Dublin again sitting in the room of a solicitors Colemans legal service regarding the death of my nan in the laundry after going through the county home. It just seemed to never stop for my family, while in the solicitors we saw a lovely woman who took all our evidence as this was the very beginning of them trying to form a case against the Irish government regarding the mother and baby homes. My mother and I sat down as she looked around the big house of the solicitors, "these was the type of houses she said" I looked around a little confused, she continued "that they would send you to on your summer holidays to clean every inch of" my eyes looked around the building, which lead up the big wideset staircase, we sat there silent in awe of the size of the house in which such a small child would take sole reasonability to clean for those members of society paying the church for slave labour. Many of whom own big retail stores in Ireland today.

We landed in Dublin and when we walked in with sweaty palms to report my nans death, we felt swamped by the size of the big room and in the distance a little window in which we approached was where a woman was sat at a desk. She looked friendly and we processed with our report, we pointed out all the factors which lead to my nans death and how my mum was brought to the laundry to be further abused. We mentioned the industrial school as it was part of the events. We quickly got the response "that was dealt with by the Ryan report" I quickly shot back the facts that the abuse was within the walls of where the industrial school was. They let us continue with why we were there regarding my nan. We were then asked regarding the Mcayleese report where I expressed their terms of just the living working residents and how it didn't address the crimes committed let alone the dead women in any manner. They called my mum back over to Ireland but instead of Dublin this time it was Cork and she provided an official statement in which we have heard nothing back from. With the history we have with the garda in regard to my mum's abuser. We are not holding out my hope.

Myself and mum then returned to Ireland alone, we planned a protest outside the Dàil, we wore matching tops and stood strong together with those we care about around as support, TDS came out from the Dáil and we were offered a meeting when we are back in Ireland but it's a little difficult to secure that meeting currently as we will not be over anytime soon as we cannot even come over for my nan. If only they acknowledged everything back when my mum brought attention to all the interlinked institutions during the Ryan report, but they didn't listen as they weren't set to gain. Now we have been the ones to have lost out more.

My mum continues to be somewhat religious and I respect her for it, many survivors even after leaving the homes still believe in god as it's all they had to hold onto in the homes. All that was there in their loneliest hour. While being beaten to death nearly in many cases. My mum doesn't want her beliefs to also be taken from her, when they also took so much. She wants change for the good people within the church because as much as there was so much bad, there was glimpses of good in some people and she continues to fight to reform the systems. I however remain spiritual, but I will never again allow my beliefs to be used by an organisation, I now nurture them myself. I will continue to write letters regarding my nan and mum and no matter how much I stay away there will forever be church and state cronies there to disturb all those in the community's journey. But from it all, I'm wiser and stronger for it and have helped my mum expose her truth and the wide extend of it. I will forever stand for the vulnerable and voiceless and I will continue to face racism for my ethnicity while trying to gain what's right for all involved. But regardless of the struggles, the emotional battering, the threats, I will continue to find the truth out further to expose to the public the full truth of the cover up in which they tried to conceal with my mum's support and I will forever be proud in the ethnicity they tried to make us ashamed in.

After launching a research project into the abuse of Irish travellers in organisations and as they left Irish institutions. On the 10th December 2018, I launched a new organisation called "Travelling people worldwide", which encourages our young and old within our community to have a political voice and to maintain our history in which has not been recorded due to prejudice. I also stripped the word Magdalene from our organisation title, and we are now known as "Justice 4 all women & children" as my nan, mum, aunt and all the women involved was not Magdalene's, they were mothers, sisters, aunts, prosecuted by the state and church. Magdalene was a word given to the women to suppress them, it's been empowering stripping their thermology.

The government are doing everything in their power to further conceal our history on the 28 February 2019 it was announced that a legislation in which I had been warning people regarding the 75-year seal had been put in place which will go against the freedom of information act. The legislation will seal the records to the child abuse inquiry and redress process. They claim it's to protect the material for further use of future scholars and generations. Yet if it was made public there could be more for them to divulge in as more survivors may come forward, they also claim that during the Ryan report they promised survivors that it will be confidential. Survivors during this point were gagged so can now not speak out about what they did and didn't agree to at the time without fear of prosecution. They are sealing the records to the child abuse inquiry and redress process as they continued to act corruptly and scam the survivor community from full justice. I have been pushing the government as well as the public to call and hold and investigation into the processes of the redress board as they based the whole proceedings on unfair trials, and this is the point in which the cover up was created. If they seal these records then no one will be able to access all the extensive evidence regarding how they continued to use and abuse rights of survivors, how they purposely excluded all the interlinked institutions, how they used exclusive commissions to hide the full extent. How the tuam burial was mentioned during the time of the Mcayleese report and they continued to suppress the truth. That was until a local historian Catherine coreless gathered some evidence through freedom of information, during this time lots of people doubted Catherine, some made lies up regarding her and said she withdrew her claims, I believed her documentation accessed by the use of freedom of information. Catholic originations came out in force to attack those who supported her. That was until the second interim report of the commission on mother and baby homes was released on the 3rd of March 2017 when the commission completed its test excavation on the tuam site. The stratigraphic survey which was conducted in October 2015 identified a particular area of interest and identified a number of sub surface anomalies that were considered a worthy of further investigation. These was further investigated by a test excavation in November/December 2016 and in January/February 2017. Test trenches were dug revealing two large structures. One structure appears to be a large sewage containment system or a septic tank that had been decommissioned and filled with rubble and debris and then covered with top soil. The second structure is a long structure which is divided into 20 chambers. The commission has not yet determined what the purpose of this structure was, but it appears to be related to the treatment/containment of sewage and/or water. The commission has also not yet determined if it was ever used for this purpose.

In this second structure, significant quantities of human remains have been discovered in at least 17 of the 20 underground chambers which were examined. A small number of remains were recovered for the purpose of analysis. These remains involved a number of individuals with the age at death ranging from 35 foetal weeks to 2-3 years. Radiocarbon dating of the samples recovered suggest that the remains date from the timeframe relevant to the operation of the mother and baby home. 9 of the mother and baby home operated from 1925 to 1961; a number of samples are likely to date from the 1950s. Further scientific tests are being conducted.

When pope Francis visited Ireland it really split the whole country, a massive remembrance for the children and women affected took place, not just in Ireland but up and down the world. From Scotland were 300 baby remains were found to America, to London where me and family walked down to a catholic church and hung baby shoes outside the door of it in remembrance of all the children. Over in Ireland my nan was remembered in Tuam, Dublin and Cork by kind members of the public as those in Ireland united to send out a clear message to the pope that we wanted change and action for all. Katherine Zappone asked the pope while on his visit if the church would contribute to the process of tuam, she has had no response. But to my family it was all a big slap in the face as we had the justice department and her ignoring my family's request of removal of my nan for years, all while now begging the church to contribute to their public display, while we are told we would have to foot all the bill and they will not help us with just gaining the permission we need. That was the hypocritical actions they took. They should both pay 50/50 to tuam processes but not for the reasoning of trying to get votes but for the reasoning of what is right and clearly, they don't want to do that as they will not help our family after making our application to the council and being completely ignored by the state and church. Their actions proved they only care for the public displays for their cover up to continue, not survivors and those affected throughout generations.

The last time my mum went to the mass grave, what use to be green grass was slushy mud and the floor was very uneven, around the grave there was a massive gap from where the stone met with the soil, my mum was shaken, she asked me if the commission could access the site without her permission, her brain also flickered to the sisters as she said "they wouldn't touch the site would they. Something just doesn't feel right all. The times I've been here and never has the ground felt like this. Maybe I'm cracking up after how much they have done to me but it all just doesn't feel right Laur", this is how they make survivors feel, that they have no control, they could do anything and survivors feel they wouldn't know if and when they did, they continuously torture our parents.

Test excavation has now begun at a burial ground and Sean ross abbey to establish if any remains are buried there by the commission. In bessborough mother and baby home Cork, remains of children are buried behind an arch way. In the wall of this arch way, nails were hammered into the wall to remember the children buried beside it. The order who own this site while the commission of investigation was taking place, without application to the local council had suddenly come to a conclusion that the arch was not safe, they had ordered builders in to completely take away the arch instead of secure it. In the middle of it all, they are disrespecting and trampling over the burial site of infants. Throughout the years the survivor community maintain what Ireland refer to as "angel plots" and mass graves of women and children, like my family, throughout the country memorial events are held. Yearly people gathered at the arch to pay their respects, this action taken without any acknowledgment this has caused great distress to the community. It made my mum say to me, "so the time when I feared them digging at my mums mass grave, really this shows they can do what they like, they own the site, they can still do what they want, they always have been allowed to and they still are" It proved in our continuous battle for justice and peace.

One day I hope to be writing a book expressing to you all regarding the day my nan is lifted from the mass grave, I always say to my family it will be a day of celebration. We want to bring my nan back to her home town mayo, where her father is buried. Keiran and his mum Marion visit mayo every year on St Patrick's day, when Keiran is done working hard, he will be like our great granddaddy returning to Ireland from the UK in the future, he promised me when the day comes for my nans freedom and he moves over he will look after her site along with her fathers. I image the day her freedom is given, and she is given all in which she is deserved by her family, to be laid to rest by those. They tried to separate us, but we found our way back together and together we will be on the day of Angelina's freedom. I hope one day this nightmare for my mum ends with the fairy tale she always deserved. Seeing her mum be respected and guided down in an old traditional horse lead wagon and to be acknowledged not excluded for who she is and acknowledged by the government as the child resident of a Magdalene laundry in which they continued to exclude and abuse.

Time is further slipping away from when I was that little girl with my note pad and pen. First approaching the dirty neglected headstone which towered over me in which I saw as my nan. But the longer this goes on, the more affected my mum becomes by them. Then the harder I plan to push for what my mum, nan, family and those alike deserves regardless. I intend to further expose the truth, record our history and most importantly keep my promise to my mum. Regardless of if I'm seen as a Tinker Menace to the society in which created me.

References:

BETTE BROWNE. 2014, *Stolen Lives,* Ireland. ISBN: 978-0-9576729-3-2.

KEVIN RYAN, 2007, Social exclusion and the politics of order.

7725
223051

||||||||| ||| | ||||| |||| ||||||| ||||
38467785R00112

Printed in Poland
by Amazon Fulfillment
Poland Sp. z o.o., Wrocław